The
Metsudah Linear

הגדה של פסח

PASSOVER
HAGGADAH

with complete instructions and explanations

by
Rabbi Avrohom Davis

Copyright © 1993
by Metsudah Publications

ISBN: 0-88125-480-0

Distributed by:

KTAV Publishing House, Inc.
900 Jefferson Street, Hoboken, NJ 07030
Tel. 201-963-9524, Fax 201-963-0102

Typography and design by:
Simcha Graphic Associates
4311 15th Avenue, Brooklyn, NY 11219
718-854-4830

יהי מצבת זכרון

לזכר נשמת משפחה הקדושים

שנהרגו על קידוש השם ביד הרוצחים ימ״ש

וגם הששה מיליון קדושים שנפלו על

קידוש השם יהי׳ זכרנם ברוכים

משפחת טויב

מענדל בן אליעזר יוסף

חי׳ה בת הירש

שמעון בן מענדל

הירש בן מענדל

יענטא בת מענדל

In memory of

our Loving Grandparents

Mr & Mrs. Berber

תנצב״ה

Zev and Ruth Fromm

Shimon & Debby

Moshe & Yitzchok

Taub

Foreword

One of the most popular books on the shelves of the Jewish library is the Pesach Haggadah. How unusual that a book which is used for only a few hours each year should be so cherished and arouse so much interest. It is difficult to establish the exact number of editions of the Haggadah but it is estimated that at least 2000 different editions of the Pesach Haggadah have been produced during the last 500 years. The appearance of yet another Haggadah would scarcely merit any attention were it not the *first Haggadah* to be produced in the *modern linear style* which has become the hallmark of Metsudah Publications.

Mah Nishtanah? How else is this Haggadah different from its predecessors? בְּכָל דּוֹר וָדוֹר חַיָּב אָדָם לִרְאוֹת אֶת עַצְמוֹ כְּאִילוּ הוּא יָצָא מִמִּצְרָיִם In each generation, every individual should feel personally redeemed from Egypt.

Therefore, each of us must tell about our personal Exodus in the language we understand, in the metaphors we use and with the knowledge we have acquired. For even if we were all scholars, all sages, all learned, we still would have to use the language of *our day* to understand, to comprehend and to relate the event of the Exodus from Egypt. This Haggadah seeks to enable *this generation of Jews* to tell about the Exodus in the clear, simple words of our daily speech while retaining the basic structure and flavor of the traditioned Haggadah.

Most of us do not have ready access to the wealth of Haggadah commentaries, and so we have carefully chosen commentaries that illuminate the text and explain its more difficult and obscure passages. We must emphasize however that this is more than just another anthology of commentaries. This Haggadah is a guide that will lead you through the Seder. We have indicated and explained the correct procedures for the performance of the mitzvos, laws and customs contained in the Haggadah, in a way that makes them more meaningful and enhances their fulfillment on the Seder night.

If this Haggadah brings a renewed measure of guidance, clarity and deeper understanding of the Seder, it will truly fulfil its purpose of magnifying and expanding the theme and keynote of the Seder: כָּל הַמַּרְבֶּה לְסַפֵּר בִּיצִיאַת מִצְרַיִם הֲרֵי זֶה מְשׁוּבָּח "Whoever amplifies the events of the exodus from Egypt deserves praise."

Introduction

One of the most familiar topics in the Pesach Haggadah is the discussion of the "four sons." According to some, this discussion is considered to be an introduction to the central theme of the Haggadah. What is the significance of the dialogue between the four sons and their father? Why is this dialogue exclusive to Pesach and specifically to the Seder night? Couldn't the questions of the four sons be directed to the observances of the other festivals?

A unique approach to the theme of the "four sons" is presented in the masterful work *Nesivos Sholom* by the revered Rebbe of Slonim, Rav Sholom Noach Berezovsky שליט״א.

בָּרוּךְ הַמָּקוֹם בָּרוּךְ הוּא, בָּרוּךְ שֶׁנָּתַן תּוֹרָה לְעַמּוֹ יִשְׂרָאֵל, בָּרוּךְ הוּא. כְּנֶגֶד אַרְבָּעָה בָנִים דִּבְּרָה תוֹרָה: אֶחָד חָכָם, וְאֶחָד רָשָׁע, וְאֶחָד תָּם, וְאֶחָד שֶׁאֵינוֹ יוֹדֵעַ לִשְׁאוֹל. "Blessed is He Who is everywhere, blessed is He. Blessed is He Who gave the Torah to His people, Israel, blessed is He."

The word בָּרוּךְ, blessed, appears four times to give thanks and praise to the Almighty, Who made mention of each of the four sons in His Torah. The fact that each son is mentioned individually indicates that regardless of his spiritual level, he is considered a בֵּן, a child of the Almighty, and whether he is a בֵּן חָכָם, a wise son, or even a בֵּן רָשָׁע, a wicked son, he is still a son and deserves a proper answer to his question.

When the wise son asks: מָה הָעֵדוֹת וְהַחֻקִּים וְהַמִּשְׁפָּטִים "What are the testimonies, and the statutes and the rules" he concludes his question with: אֲשֶׁר צִוָּה ה' א-קינו אֶתְכֶם "which Adony, our God has commanded you." The word צִוָּה command, is similar to the word צַוְותָּא, which implies joining or clinging, for the optimal result of a מִצְוָה, a command, is the forging of a bond linking man to God.

The wise son asks "How is it that the righteous (צַדִּיקִים) are able to forge a bond with God through their observance of the מִצְוֹת the commands, and I who also observe them do not feel this attachment or closeness to Him? The answer to his

ix

question is: וְאַף אַתָּה אֱמֹר לוֹ כְּהִלְכוֹת הַפֶּסַח, אֵין מַפְטִירִין אַחַר הַפֶּסַח אֲפִיקוֹמָן
"Explain to him that the regulations of Pesach require that
nothing be eaten after the *afikoman*." The law is that הַפֶּסַח נֶאֱכָל
עַל הַשֹּׂבַע, the Pesach sacrifice, the Paschal lamb must be eaten
on a full stomach. The person must be completely satiated
before partaking of the קָרְבַּן פֶּסַח. Obviously one does not find
enjoyment or pleasure from food that he eats on a full stomach.
The mitzvah to eat of the Pesach offering was not intended as
a gastronomical treat, on the contrary, one was not supposed
to experience material pleasure from it. Thus the wise son is
taught that after the *afikoman* which in our time is in place of
the *Korban* Pesach, and thus is eaten after the full meal, we are
not permitted to eat any other food. The taste of the *afikoman*
must remain in our mouths through the night. Similarly, he
is to understand that in order to experience closeness to the
Eternal through the performance of *mitzvos,* he must minimize
any worldly or secular benefit that might be derived through
them, so that the pure spirit of the mitzvah is undiluted by any
material benefit.

The בֵּן רָשָׁע, the wicked son, does not describe a son who
has left the fold and gone astray. Rather it refers to a son who
has given up in despair because of the obstacles and pitfalls he
has encountered along the path, leading to a genuine Torah
way of life. His question is, how is it that you have survived,
and merited Divine support to strengthen your committment
and service to the Almighty? How can I serve Him when I
am in constant turmoil and in conflict with the *Yeitzer Horah*?
How can I make a committment to serve Him when I have
despaired of overcoming my doubts and my shortcomings?
The answer to his question is: אִלּוּ הָיָה שָׁם לֹא הָיָה נִגְאָל. "Had you
been there you would not have been redeemed." He is told
when we were in Egypt, we were sunken and mired in the
depths of the מ"ט שַׁעֲרֵי טוּמְאָה, the forty-ninth level of impurity,
and yet we did not give up or lose hope of spiritual redemption
as well as physical redemption. If we had despaired because
of our spiritual deterioration, we would not have merited the

spiritial rejuvenation that came with our release from physical bondage. "Thus if you were there you would not have been redeemed."

He is taught the lesson of hope and faith. So long as there is a spark of *yiddishkeit,* Judaism, be it ever so dim, there is always salvation for him.

The תָּם, the "simple" son, refers to the son who is apathetic or indifferent to the whole idea of serving God. He is so totally removed from the concept of anything Divine that all he can ask is "מַה זֹּאת, what is this all about?" (It has been observed that the letters of תָּם are the same as the letters of מֵת, death, which implies that the תָּם is one who is not alive in regard to spiritial matters.) The answer to his question is therefore: "בְּחוֹזֶק יָד הוֹצִיאָנוּ ה׳ מִמִּצְרַיִם, with a mighty hand did God take us out of Egypt." We say to him that only with tremendous energy and effort can he be aroused from his lethargic state of mind to which he is chained. His redemption depends on awakening the latent power of his *neshamah,* the Divine soul within him.

The שֶׁאֵינוֹ יוֹדֵעַ לִשְׁאוֹל, the son who does not know enough to ask, is one whose intellectual and emotional faculties have not developed. He is so "closed in" that he lacks the curiosity to ask even the most elementary and obvious questions. The Torah therefore advises his parent: וְהִגַּדְתָּ לְבִנְךָ בַּיּוֹם הַהוּא לֵאמֹר בַּעֲבוּר זֶה עָשָׂה ה׳ לִי בְּצֵאתִי מִמִּצְרַיִם "And you shall explain to your son on that day, saying, 'This is done because of what God did for me when I went out of Egypt.'" Tell your son that when we were enslaved in Egypt, we too were undeveloped and "closed in" to such an extent that the Sages referred to our situation as כְּמוֹ עוּבָּר בִּמְעֵי בְהֵמָה like an unborn fetus in its mother's womb. We were so phlegmatic that we had to be extracted from Egypt through Divine power. The only thing we had going for ourselves was our אֱמוּנָה, our faith in the God of our fathers, and so even now with faith we too can hope that our hearts and minds will be opened to receive the Divine light of Torah.

In summation, the Torah teaches us about the "four sons" specifically on Pesach because through the message of Pesach all of them can be uplifted and inspired, each of them according to their level of understanding and desire. Even the so-called בֶּן רָשָׁע can be encouraged through the majesty of the Seder night.

Since we are all referred to as בָּנִים לַמָּקוֹם, children of His majesty, the Holy One blessed is He, we are confident that complete salvation and redemption of our bodies and souls will soon be a reality.

הגדה של פסח

PASSOVER
HAGGADAH

All preparations for the seder should be completed by the time synagogue services are finished. The matzos and the other symbolic items should be placed on the table in the following arrangement.

ג׳ מצות
3 Matzos

The Search for Chometz   בְּדִיקַת חָמֵץ

On the evening of the day before Pesach, the search for leaven, *bedikas chometz,* is conducted. This is a mitzvah which symbolizes the final cleaning of the house of all *chometz.* Usually the head of the family performs the mitzvah by searching the entire house thoroughly for *chometz.* (When the first day of Pesach is on Sunday, the search is conducted on the previous Thursday night.) To facilitate the search, it is customary to place pieces of bread in various rooms around the house. (Remember how many pieces there are and where they were hidden.) The search is traditionally conducted with a candle for light and with a feather and wooden spoon to collect the *chometz.*

Before you begin the search, light the candle, and say:

Blessed are You, Adonoy	בָּרוּךְ אַתָּה יְיָ,
our God, King of the Universe,	אֱלֹהֵינוּ מֶלֶךְ הָעוֹלָם,
Who sanctified us with His commandments	אֲשֶׁר קִדְּשָׁנוּ בְּמִצְוֹתָיו,
and commanded us to remove all *chometz.*	וְצִוָּנוּ עַל־בִּעוּר חָמֵץ:

After the search, any chometz which may have escaped detection is nullified with the following declaration:

All *chometz,* leaven and unleavened bread	כָּל־חֲמִירָא וַחֲמִיעָא,
in my possession	דְּאִכָּא בִּרְשׁוּתִי,
which I have not seen and not removed,	דְּלָא חֲמִתֵּהּ, וּדְלָא בְעַרְתֵּהּ,

1

and of which I am unaware,	וּדְלָא יְדַעְנָא לֵהּ,
is hereby nullified and ownerless	לִבְטִיל וְלֶהֱוֵי הֶפְקֵר,
as the dust of the earth.	כְּעַפְרָא דְאַרְעָא:

On erev Pesach, you may eat *chometz* until about 9:00 A.M. As this time varies from year to year, you should consult your Rabbi for the exact time. Within the hour that follows, the burning of the *chometz* must take place.

After burning the chometz the following declaration is made:

All *chometz*, leaven and unleavened bread	כָּל־חֲמִירָא וַחֲמִיעָא,
in my possession	דְּאִכָּא בִרְשׁוּתִי,
whether I have seen it or not,	דַּחֲזִתֵּהּ וּדְלָא חֲזִתֵּהּ,
whether I have removed it or not,	דְּבִעַרְתֵּהּ וּדְלָא בִעַרְתֵּהּ,
is hereby nullified and ownerless,	לִבְטִיל וְלֶהֱוֵי הֶפְקֵר,
as the dust of the earth.	כְּעַפְרָא דְאַרְעָא:

When the 2nd day of Pesach is on Friday, a problem arises concerning the preparation of food for Shabbos. While it is permitted to cook on Yom Tov, it is forbidden to cook and prepare food on Yom Tov for Shabbos. Therefore, since Yom Tov is Thursday and Friday (and since on Shabbos itself cooking is forbidden), it would be impossible to cook any food for Shabbos. However, the Sages ruled that if the preparation is begun before Yom Tov, that is, on Wednesday, it can be continued during Yom Tov. Therefore, the problem can be solved with the mitzvah of *eiruv tavshilin*. Some cooked food and matzoh are set aside to be eaten on Shabbos, thereby permitting the preparation of additional food for Shabbos during Yom Tov.

Eiruv Tavshilin עֵירוּב תַּבְשִׁילִין

When the 2nd day of Pesach is on Friday, an eiruv tavshilin must be prepared on the preceding Wednesday. The head of the family should take some matzoh and some cooked food such as meat or fish, put them on a plate and say the following berachah:

Blessed are You, Adonoy,	בָּרוּךְ אַתָּה יְיָ
our God, King of the Universe	אֱלֹהֵינוּ מֶלֶךְ הָעוֹלָם,
Who sanctified us with His commandments	אֲשֶׁר קִדְּשָׁנוּ בְּמִצְוֹתָיו
and commanded us	וְצִוָּנוּ
concerning the mitzvah of *eiruv*.	עַל־מִצְוַת עֵרוּב:

By means of this *eiruv*	בַּהֲדֵין עֵרוּבָא
it will be permissible for us to bake,	יְהֵא שָׁרֵא לָנָא לְאָפוּיֵי
cook, keep dishes warm,[1]	וּלְבַשּׁוּלֵי, וּלְאַצְלוּיֵי, וּלְאַטְמוּנֵי,
to kindle a light (from an existing flame),	וּלְאַדְלוּקֵי שְׁרָגָא,
and to prepare and do all our necessities	וּלְתַקָּנָא, וּלְמֶעְבַּד כָּל־צָרְכָנָא,
on the Festival for the needs of Shabbos,	מִיּוֹמָא טָבָא לְשַׁבַּתָּא,
for us and for all Jews[2]	לָנוּ, וּלְכָל־יִשְׂרָאֵל,
who live in this city.	הַדָּרִים בָּעִיר הַזֹּאת:

The food of the eiruv should be eaten at one of the Shabbos meals.

---

[1] "Keeping dishes warm" means that we are permitted to place *cooked foods* on a *covered* stove in order to preserve their heat. An example of this is the traditional Cholent. Kindling of light refers to the transferral of fire from an existing fire.

[2] The Rav of the community usually includes the community in his *eiruv*. This can be done however by anyone. It is done by handing over the cooked food to another person through whom he grants a share of the food (of the *eiruv*) to the entire community. This person raises the *eiruv* a *tefach* (handsbreadth) and returns it to the one making the *eiruv*.

Lighting the Candles · הַדְלָקַת הַגֵּרוֹת

Blessed are You, Adonoy,
our God, King of the Universe
Who sanctified us with His commandments
and commanded us
to kindle the Festival light.

בָּרוּךְ אַתָּה יְיָ,
אֱלֹהֵינוּ מֶלֶךְ הָעוֹלָם,
אֲשֶׁר קִדְּשָׁנוּ בְּמִצְוֹתָיו,
וְצִוָּנוּ
לְהַדְלִיק נֵר שֶׁל יוֹם טוֹב:

Blessed are You, Adonoy,
our God, King of the Universe
Who has kept us alive and sustained us
and brought us to this season.

בָּרוּךְ אַתָּה יְיָ,
אֱלֹהֵינוּ מֶלֶךְ הָעוֹלָם,
שֶׁהֶחֱיָנוּ, וְקִיְּמָנוּ, וְהִגִּיעָנוּ
לַזְּמַן הַזֶּה:

When Yom Tov occurs on Shabbos:

Blessed are You, Adonoy,
our God, King of the Universe
Who sanctified us with His commandments
and commanded us
to kindle the Shabbos light
and Festival light.

בָּרוּךְ אַתָּה יְיָ,
אֱלֹהֵינוּ מֶלֶךְ הָעוֹלָם,
אֲשֶׁר קִדְּשָׁנוּ בְּמִצְוֹתָיו,
וְצִוָּנוּ
לְהַדְלִיק נֵר שֶׁל שַׁבָּת
וְיוֹם טוֹב:

Blessed are You, Adonoy,
our God, King of the Universe
Who has kept us alive and sustained us
and brought us to this season.

בָּרוּךְ אַתָּה יְיָ,
אֱלֹהֵינוּ מֶלֶךְ הָעוֹלָם,
שֶׁהֶחֱיָנוּ, וְקִיְּמָנוּ, וְהִגִּיעָנוּ
לַזְּמַן הַזֶּה:

Order of the Pesach Seder · סִימָנֵי הַסֵּדֶר

Kadeish, Urchatz, Karpas, Yachatz,
Maggid, Rochtzah, Motzi Matzoh,
Morror, Koreich, Shulchan Orech,
Tzafun, Bareich, Hallel, Nirtzah.

קַדֵּשׁ. וּרְחַץ. כַּרְפַּס. יַחַץ.
מַגִּיד. רָחְצָה. מוֹצִיא. מַצָּה.
מָרוֹר. כּוֹרֵךְ. שֻׁלְחָן עוֹרֵךְ.
צָפוּן. בָּרֵךְ. הַלֵּל. נִרְצָה.

Kadeish (Kiddush) קַדֵּשׁ

The cups are filled. Each cup must hold a minimum of 3.3 ounces of wine. Some authorities maintain that 5.3 ounces is the minimum. You should drink more than half the cup of wine each of the four times that the wine is drunk at the Seder. If possible, you should drink the entire cup each time.

At this time, some have the custom to pour an extra cup of wine called the Cup of Elijah. Others, however, do so after drinking the third cup, (after *Birchas Hamazon*). The head of the household or the leader of the Seder should not fill his own cup nor do any serving. As a sign of freedom, he is to be waited upon by others.

When Pesach occurs on Shabbos, begin here:

Recite quietly:

And evening came, and morning came:	וַיְהִי־עֶרֶב וַיְהִי־בֹקֶר

Recite aloud:

the sixth day.	יוֹם הַשִּׁשִּׁי:
And the heavens and the earth were completed	וַיְכֻלּוּ, הַשָּׁמַיִם וְהָאָרֶץ
and [so were] all their hosts.	וְכָל־צְבָאָם:
And God completed, by the seventh day,	וַיְכַל אֱלֹהִים בַּיּוֹם הַשְּׁבִיעִי,
His work which He had done;	מְלַאכְתּוֹ אֲשֶׁר עָשָׂה,
and He abstained on the seventh day	וַיִּשְׁבֹּת בַּיּוֹם הַשְּׁבִיעִי,
from all His work which He had done.	מִכָּל־מְלַאכְתּוֹ אֲשֶׁר עָשָׂה:
And God blessed the seventh day	וַיְבָרֶךְ אֱלֹהִים אֶת־יוֹם הַשְּׁבִיעִי,
and sanctified it,	וַיְקַדֵּשׁ אֹתוֹ,
for on it He abstained	כִּי בוֹ שָׁבַת
from all His work	מִכָּל־מְלַאכְתּוֹ,
which God had created to do.	אֲשֶׁר־בָּרָא אֱלֹהִים לַעֲשׂוֹת:

When Pesach occurs on a weekday, begin here:

Attention! our masters and our teachers:	סַבְרִי מָרָנָן וְרַבּוֹתַי:
Blessed are You, Adonoy,	בָּרוּךְ אַתָּה יְיָ,
our God, King of the Universe,	אֱלֹהֵינוּ מֶלֶךְ הָעוֹלָם,
Creator of the fruit of the vine.	בּוֹרֵא, פְּרִי הַגָּפֶן:

Blessed are You, Adonoy,	בָּרוּךְ אַתָּה יְיָ,
our God, King of the Universe	אֱלֹהֵינוּ מֶלֶךְ הָעוֹלָם,
Who chose us from among all people,	אֲשֶׁר בָּחַר בָּנוּ מִכָּל־עָם,
and exalted us above all (tongues) languages,	וְרוֹמְמָנוּ מִכָּל־לָשׁוֹן,
and sanctified us with His commandments.	וְקִדְּשָׁנוּ בְּמִצְוֹתָיו,
And [You] gave us, Adonoy, our God,	וַתִּתֶּן לָנוּ יְיָ אֱלֹהֵינוּ
in love	בְּאַהֲבָה

Add on Shabbos:

Shabbos days for rest, and	שַׁבָּתוֹת לִמְנוּחָה וּ

appointed festivals for rejoicing,	מוֹעֲדִים לְשִׂמְחָה,
festivals and seasons for happiness,	חַגִּים וּזְמַנִּים לְשָׂשׂוֹן,
this day of	אֶת־יוֹם

Add on Shabbos:

Shabbos, and	הַשַּׁבָּת הַזֶּה, וְאֶת־יוֹם

this Festival of Matzos,	חַג הַמַּצּוֹת הַזֶּה.
the season of our freedom,	זְמַן חֵרוּתֵנוּ,

Add on Shabbos:

with love	בְּאַהֲבָה

a day of holy assembly	מִקְרָא קֹדֶשׁ,
commemorating the exodus from Egypt.	זֵכֶר לִיצִיאַת מִצְרָיִם.
For us have You chosen	כִּי בָנוּ בָחַרְתָּ,
and us have You sanctified	וְאוֹתָנוּ קִדַּשְׁתָּ,
from among all peoples,	מִכָּל־הָעַמִּים.

Add on Shabbos:

and Shabbos	וְשַׁבָּת

and Your appointed festivals of holiness	וּמוֹעֲדֵי קָדְשֶׁךָ

Add on Shabbos:

with love and pleasure	בְּאַהֲבָה וּבְרָצוֹן

in joy and in happiness	בְּשִׂמְחָה וּבְשָׂשׂוֹן
You gave us for a heritage.	הִנְחַלְתָּנוּ:
Blessed are You, Adonoy,	בָּרוּךְ אַתָּה יְיָ,
Sanctifier of	מְקַדֵּשׁ

Add on Shabbos:

Shabbos, and	הַשַּׁבָּת וְ

Israel and the seasons.	יִשְׂרָאֵל וְהַזְּמַנִּים:

You must drink the wine while reclining on your left side.
On Saturday night, see instruction on page 8.

Blessed are You, Adonoy,	בָּרוּךְ אַתָּה יְיָ,
our God, King of the Universe	אֱלֹהֵינוּ מֶלֶךְ הָעוֹלָם,
Who has kept us alive and sustained us	שֶׁהֶחֱיָנוּ, וְקִיְּמָנוּ, וְהִגִּיעָנוּ,
and brought us to this season.	לַזְּמַן הַזֶּה:

When Yom Tov occurs at the conclusion of Shabbos,
the following two berachos are said
before the beracha of "שֶׁהֶחֱיָנוּ, Who has kept us alive:"

Blessed are You, Adonoy,   בָּרוּךְ אַתָּה יְיָ,

our God, King of the Universe   אֱלֹהֵינוּ מֶלֶךְ הָעוֹלָם,

Creator of the lights of fire.   בּוֹרֵא, מְאוֹרֵי הָאֵשׁ:

Blessed are You, Adonoy,   בָּרוּךְ אַתָּה יְיָ

our God, King of the Universe   אֱלֹהֵינוּ מֶלֶךְ הָעוֹלָם,

Who has made a distinction   הַמַּבְדִּיל בֵּין

between the sacred and the unhallowed,   קֹדֶשׁ לְחוֹל,

between light and darkness,   בֵּין אוֹר לְחֹשֶׁךְ,

between Israel and the peoples,   בֵּין יִשְׂרָאֵל לָעַמִּים,

between the seventh day   בֵּין יוֹם הַשְּׁבִיעִי

and the six work days.   לְשֵׁשֶׁת יְמֵי הַמַּעֲשֶׂה.

Between the sanctity of Shabbos   בֵּין קְדֻשַּׁת שַׁבָּת

and the sanctity of Yom Tov   לִקְדֻשַּׁת יוֹם טוֹב

You have distinguished,   הִבְדַּלְתָּ.

and the seventh day   וְאֶת־יוֹם הַשְּׁבִיעִי

[from] the six work days You have sanctified.   מִשֵּׁשֶׁת יְמֵי הַמַּעֲשֶׂה קִדַּשְׁתָּ.

You have distinguished and sanctified   הִבְדַּלְתָּ וְקִדַּשְׁתָּ

Your people Israel with holiness.   אֶת־עַמְּךָ יִשְׂרָאֵל בִּקְדֻשָּׁתֶךָ:

Blessed are You, Adonoy,   בָּרוּךְ אַתָּה יְיָ,

Who distinguishes between sacred and sacred.   הַמַּבְדִּיל בֵּין־קֹדֶשׁ לְקֹדֶשׁ:

You must drink the wine while reclining on your left side.

Urchatz וּרְחַץ

*Water is brought to the table for the head of the household
or the Seder leader and he washes his hands.
The others may wash their hands in the usual place.
The regular berachah for washing the hands* (Netilas Yodaim)
is not said at this time.

The hands are washed for the following reason: Whenever food is dipped into a liquid and eaten while it is wet, the hands must be washed. Since the Karpas is about to be dipped in salt water, we therefore must wash our hands.

Karpas כַּרְפַּס

In order to stimulate the children to ask questions, something out of the ordinary is done at the beginning of the Seder. (Tradition prescribes, for example, the distribution of nuts to the children.) A vegetable is taken and dipped into salt water. This particular type of food was chosen for the Seder in order to say the berachah, BO-RE P'RI HO-ADOMO, which includes the *marror* which is eaten later.

Therefore, for Karpas you may take parsley, radishes, celery, potato, etc. (anything over which the berachah BO-RE P'RI HO-ADOMO can be said). Also, only a small quantity should be eaten (less than a *k'zayis*, 1/2 egg-volume) so as not to necessitate a concluding blessing after it.

*The eating of the Karpas does not require reclining.
Before eating the Karpas, the following berachah is said:*

Blessed are You Adonoy,	בָּרוּךְ אַתָּה יְיָ,
our God, King of the universe	אֱלֹהֵינוּ מֶלֶךְ הָעוֹלָם,
who creates fruit of the earth.	בּוֹרֵא, פְּרִי הָאֲדָמָה:

Yachatz　יַחַץ

The Seder leader takes the middle Matzoh
from the Seder plate and breaks it into two pieces.
The smaller piece he puts back on the Seder plate.
He wraps the larger piece in a napkin and puts it aside.
This is to be used for the Afikomon at the end of the Seder meal.

The Matzoh is broken to emphasize that it is the "Bread of Affliction." A poor man does not know whence his daily bread comes and usually doesn't even possess a whole loaf of bread. If he is fortunate in acquiring a full loaf of bread, he will not eat it all on the same day, but will keep part of it for another day. So too we symbolize our "Bread of Affliction" in this manner.

The Afikomon traditionally plays an exciting role with the children. In order to keep them awake and interested in the Seder, children are encouraged to try to remove the Afikomon secretly, hide it, and hold it for a ransom.

Maggid　מַגִּיד

With the following paragraphs, the Haggadah recital begins. It is customary to remove the bone and egg from the Seder plate. (Some do this after HO LACHMO ANYO.) The Matzos are uncovered and the Seder plate is lifted by the Seder participants, while HO LACHMO ANYO is recited.

In ancient times, it was common practice to remove the Seder plate entirely from the table, in order to arouse the children's curiosity. They are accustomed to being served the meal after having listened to Kiddush on Shabbos or Yom Tov evening, and when they see that instead of food being served, the plate is removed, they will ask questions. The idea is further enhanced when the piece of Matzoh for the Afikomon is put aside, and when the bone and egg are removed from the Seder plate, which is now lifted.

The Bread of Affliction — הָא לַחְמָא עַנְיָא

This was the bread of affliction[3]	הָא לַחְמָא עַנְיָא,
which our ancestors ate	דִּי אֲכָלוּ אַבְהָתָנָא
while they were enslaved in Egypt.	בְּאַרְעָא דְמִצְרָיִם.
All who are hungry—let them come and eat,	כָּל־דִּכְפִין יֵיתֵי וְיֵכוֹל,
all who are in need—	כָּל־דִּצְרִיךְ
let them come and join us for the Pesach Seder.	יֵיתֵי וְיִפְסַח.
For the present we are here,	הָשַׁתָּא הָכָא,
but next year we will be in Eretz Yisroel.	לְשָׁנָה הַבָּאָה בְּאַרְעָא דְיִשְׂרָאֵל.
For the present we are still in servitude,	הָשַׁתָּא עַבְדֵי,
but next year we hope to be truly free men.	לְשָׁנָה הַבָּאָה בְּנֵי חוֹרִין:

The second cup is filled.
The Matzos are covered.
The child asks the four questions.

(It is customary that the youngest child recites the MA NISHTANO. If no child is present, any Seder participant may recite it. Even when a person conducts the Seder for himself he asks the questions, for the order, fixed by our Sages may not be changed.)

---

[3] Matzoh is called the bread of affliction because a) it is lowly, since without yeast, it lacks the ingredient which makes bread rise. b) it was fed to slaves, since it takes longer to digest and, thus, is filling. c) it is baked quickly in the fashion of the poor, who try to conserve fuel.

The Four Questions   מַה נִּשְׁתַּנָּה

How different is this night   מַה נִּשְׁתַּנָּה הַלַּיְלָה הַזֶּה,

from all other nights!   מִכָּל־הַלֵּילוֹת?

On all other nights,   שֶׁבְּכָל הַלֵּילוֹת,

we eat *chometz* or *matzoh*.   אָנוּ אוֹכְלִין חָמֵץ וּמַצָּה,

Why on this night, do we eat only matzoh?   הַלַּיְלָה הַזֶּה כֻּלּוֹ מַצָּה:

On all other nights   שֶׁבְּכָל הַלֵּילוֹת

we eat all kinds of vegetables.   אָנוּ אוֹכְלִין שְׁאָר יְרָקוֹת,

Why on this night, do we eat bitter herbs?   הַלַּיְלָה הַזֶּה (כֻּלּוֹ) מָרוֹר:

On all other nights   שֶׁבְּכָל הַלֵּילוֹת

we do not dip (vegetables)   אֵין אָנוּ מַטְבִּילִין,

even once (during the meal).   אֲפִלּוּ פַּעַם אֶחָת,

Why on this night, do we dip twice?   הַלַּיְלָה הַזֶּה שְׁתֵּי פְעָמִים:

On all other nights we eat   שֶׁבְּכָל הַלֵּילוֹת, אָנוּ אוֹכְלִין,

either sitting upright or reclining.   בֵּין יוֹשְׁבִין, וּבֵין מְסֻבִּין,

Why on this night, do we eat reclining?   הַלַּיְלָה הַזֶּה כֻּלָּנוּ מְסֻבִּין:

The Matzos are uncovered.

Throughout the Haggadah recital, the Matzos remain uncovered, especially when a paragraph deals with the Matzoh. However, when the cup of wine is lifted, the Matzos are covered.

According to the order of berachos, bread has preference over wine. Therefore, whenever wine is taken in hand on Pesach, the Matzoh should be covered in order not to "slight" it.

The wine also symbolizes our freedom while the Matzoh reminds us of our former bondage. Therefore, we cover one while raising the other.

With the following paragraph we begin to answer the four questions asked in the MA NISHTANO.

The Reply   הַתְּשׁוּבָה

We were slaves to Pharaoh in Egypt[4]	עֲבָדִים הָיִינוּ לְפַרְעֹה בְּמִצְרַיִם,
but Adonoy, our God took us out of there	וַיּוֹצִיאֵנוּ יְיָ אֱלֹהֵינוּ מִשָּׁם,
with a mighty hand and outstretched arm.	בְּיָד חֲזָקָה וּבִזְרֹעַ נְטוּיָה,
Had not	וְאִלּוּ לֹא
the Holy One, blessed is He, taken out	הוֹצִיא, הַקָּדוֹשׁ בָּרוּךְ הוּא,
our ancestors from Egypt,	אֶת־אֲבוֹתֵינוּ מִמִּצְרַיִם,
then we, our children, and our grandchildren	הֲרֵי אָנוּ, וּבָנֵינוּ וּבְנֵי בָנֵינוּ,
would still be enslaved	מְשֻׁעְבָּדִים הָיִינוּ
by a Pharaoh in Egypt.	לְפַרְעֹה בְּמִצְרָיִם,
Thus, even if all of us were scholars,	וַאֲפִלּוּ כֻּלָּנוּ חֲכָמִים,
all of us sages, all of us elders,	כֻּלָּנוּ נְבוֹנִים, כֻּלָּנוּ זְקֵנִים,
all of us learned in Torah,	כֻּלָּנוּ יוֹדְעִים אֶת־הַתּוֹרָה,
we would still be required	מִצְוָה עָלֵינוּ
to tell the story of the Exodus from Egypt.	לְסַפֵּר בִּיצִיאַת מִצְרָיִם.
and whoever amplifies upon the events	וְכָל־הַמַּרְבֶּה לְסַפֵּר
associated with the Exodus from Egypt	בִּיצִיאַת מִצְרַיִם
deserves praise.	הֲרֵי זֶה מְשֻׁבָּח:

The following two narratives of the Tannaim Sages illustrate the praiseworthiness of expanding upon the theme of the Exodus from Egypt.

---

[4] We now begin the central section of the Haggadah. The questions of *Mah Nishtanah* are not answered directly, but the source material for the answers are provided. The structure here follows the principle stated in the Talmud: "We begin [the Haggadah] with degradation and conclude with praise" (*Pesachim* 116a). The precise meaning of degradation referred to is a subject of debate between Rav and Shmuel. Shmuel is of the opinion that degradation refers to physical slavery; thus, we should recite the section beginning "עבדים היינו, We were slaves." Rav maintains that degradation refers to idolatry and suggests using the section beginning, "At the beginning our ancestors served idols." Traditionally, both sections are used, and as we have it, it is a movement from physical enslavement to spiritual enslavement and is followed by total redemption from both.

There is a story about Rabbi Eliezer, מַעֲשֶׂה בְּרַבִּי אֱלִיעֶזֶר,

Rabbi Yehoshua, וְרַבִּי יְהוֹשֻׁעַ,

Rabbi Elazar ben Azariah, וְרַבִּי אֶלְעָזָר בֶּן־עֲזַרְיָה,

Rabbi Akiva and Rabbi Tarfon וְרַבִּי עֲקִיבָא, וְרַבִּי טַרְפוֹן,

who had assembled in Bnei Brak.[5] שֶׁהָיוּ מְסֻבִּין בִּבְנֵי־בְרַק,

They were so absorbed in telling וְהָיוּ מְסַפְּרִים

the story of the Exodus from Egypt[6] בִּיצִיאַת מִצְרַיִם,

that the entire night passed[7] כָּל־אוֹתוֹ הַלַּיְלָה,

when their disciples came over[8] עַד שֶׁבָּאוּ תַלְמִידֵיהֶם

and said to them; "Our Masters, it is time וְאָמְרוּ לָהֶם: רַבּוֹתֵינוּ, הִגִּיעַ זְמַן

to recite the morning *Shemah*." קְרִיאַת שְׁמַע, שֶׁל שַׁחֲרִית:

Rabbi Elazar ben Azariah said, אָמַר רַבִּי אֶלְעָזָר בֶּן־עֲזַרְיָה.

"Although I am like a seventy-year-old man[9] הֲרֵי אֲנִי כְּבֶן שִׁבְעִים שָׁנָה,

I was never privileged וְלֹא זָכִיתִי,

that the story of the Exodus be recited שֶׁתֵּאָמֵר יְצִיאַת מִצְרַיִם

at night,[10] בַּלֵּילוֹת.

until Ben Zoma interpreted the verse,[11] עַד שֶׁדְּרָשָׁהּ בֶּן זוֹמָא.

'In order that you may remember שֶׁנֶּאֱמַר: לְמַעַן תִּזְכֹּר,

the day of your departure from Egypt אֶת־יוֹם צֵאתְךָ מֵאֶרֶץ מִצְרַיִם,

all the days of your life?' כֹּל יְמֵי חַיֶּיךָ.

the *days* of your life imply merely the daytime, יְמֵי חַיֶּיךָ הַיָּמִים.

but *all* the days of your life כֹּל יְמֵי חַיֶּיךָ

[5] They had gathered together to celebrate the first night of Pesach.
[6] They were deeply involved in re-telling the story of the Exodus in great detail.
[7] Without their being aware of it.
[8] To interrupt them.
[9] His hair had turned white prematurely.
[10] He was never privileged to find valid Biblical support for reciting the story of the Exodus at night.
[11] *Devarim* 16:3.

clearly imply the nights."[12]	הַלֵּילוֹת.
The Sages interpreted this verse saying,	וַחֲכָמִים אוֹמְרִים:
'The days of your life refer to this world,	יְמֵי חַיֶּיךָ הָעוֹלָם הַזֶּה.
all the days of your life indicates	כֹּל יְמֵי חַיֶּיךָ
that the Messianic era is also included.	לְהָבִיא לִימוֹת הַמָּשִׁיחַ:

Blessed is He Who is everywhere,	בָּרוּךְ הַמָּקוֹם.
Blessed is He	בָּרוּךְ הוּא.
Blessed is He who gave the Torah	בָּרוּךְ שֶׁנָּתַן תּוֹרָה
to His people Israel, Blessed is He.	לְעַמּוֹ יִשְׂרָאֵל. בָּרוּךְ הוּא.

The Four Sons   אַרְבָּעָה בָנִים

It is concerning four types of sons	כְּנֶגֶד אַרְבָּעָה בָנִים
that the Torah speaks:	דִּבְּרָה תוֹרָה.
one is wise and one is wicked,	אֶחָד חָכָם, וְאֶחָד רָשָׁע,
and one is quite simple,	וְאֶחָד תָּם,
and one who does not know enough to ask.	וְאֶחָד שֶׁאֵינוֹ יוֹדֵעַ לִשְׁאוֹל:

What does the wise son ask?	חָכָם מָה הוּא אוֹמֵר
He asks: "What are the testimonies,	מָה הָעֵדֹת
statutes and rules	וְהַחֻקִּים וְהַמִּשְׁפָּטִים,
which Adonoy, *our* God has commanded you?"[13]	אֲשֶׁר צִוָּה יְיָ אֱלֹהֵינוּ אֶתְכֶם
and you should explain to him[14]	וְאַף אַתָּה אֱמָר־לוֹ

---

[12] Since the Torah prefixed the word כל, *all* to this phrase, the addition of this word clearly implies that the nights are also to be included.

[13] *Devorim* 6:20.

[14] Since he has asked an intelligent, proper and valid question, so should you, too, respond in the same manner and in your reply include the explanation of the entire scope of the Pesach laws, even to the law . . .

all the Pesach laws and regulations	כְּהִלְכוֹת הַפֶּסַח:
[even to the extent of this final law].	
Nothing should be eaten after	אֵין מַפְטִירִין אַחַר הַפֶּסַח
the *Afikomon*.[15]	אֲפִיקוֹמָן:

What does the wicked son ask?	רָשָׁע מָה הוּא אוֹמֵר
[He asks]: "What is the ritual of *yours*"?[16]	מָה הָעֲבוֹדָה הַזֹּאת לָכֶם
Yours he emphasizes but not *his*,	לָכֶם וְלֹא לוֹ.
Because he excludes himself	וּלְפִי שֶׁהוֹצִיא אֶת־עַצְמוֹ
from the community,	מִן הַכְּלָל,
and denies the principle to acknowledge God,	כָּפַר בְּעִקָּר.
so should you dull the sharpness of his sarcasm	וְאַף אַתָּה הַקְהֵה אֶת־שִׁנָּיו,
and reply to him,	וֶאֱמָר־לוֹ:
"This is because of what Adonoy did for *me*	בַּעֲבוּר זֶה, עָשָׂה יְיָ לִי,
when I went out of Egypt."[17]	בְּצֵאתִי מִמִּצְרָיִם.
[He did it] for *me* and not for *him*.	לִי וְלֹא־לוֹ.
Had he been there	אִלּוּ הָיָה שָׁם,
he would not have been redeemed.[18]	לֹא הָיָה נִגְאָל:

What does the simple son ask?	תָּם מָה הוּא אוֹמֵר
[He asks:] What is this all about?[19]	מַה זֹּאת

[15] In its original form, the law meant that nothing should be eaten after the Pesach offering. This law is among the last dealt with in the tenth chapter of *Maseches Pesachim*, which discusses the laws of the Seder. Today, because we no longer have a Pesach sacrifice, the rule has come to mean that nothing should be eaten after the *afikoman* matzoh, so its taste (like that of the Pesach sacrifice) can linger in our mouths.

[16] *Shemos* 12:26.

[17] *Shemos* 13:8. The response to the wicked son is "me and not him" rather than "me and not you," because the parent is speaking to the others. He knows that there is no point in speaking further to the wicked son.

[18] The response to the wicked child is not done out of malice. Rather, it is an attempt to shock him, so that he will repent and change his ways.

[19] His question is asked out of pure innocence.

You shall say to him,	וְאָמַרְתָּ אֵלָיו:
"With a mighty hand	בְּחֹזֶק יָד
Adonoy took us out of Egypt	הוֹצִיאָנוּ יְיָ מִמִּצְרַיִם
out of the house of bondage."[20]	מִבֵּית עֲבָדִים:

As for the child who does not know	וְשֶׁאֵינוֹ יוֹדֵעַ
enough to ask,	לִשְׁאוֹל,
you should begin for him, as it is said,	אַתְּ פְּתַח לוֹ. שֶׁנֶּאֱמַר:
"And you shall relate [explain] to your son	וְהִגַּדְתָּ לְבִנְךָ,
on that day saying:	בַּיּוֹם הַהוּא לֵאמֹר:
'Because of this did Adonoy do for me	בַּעֲבוּר זֶה עָשָׂה יְיָ לִי,
when I went out of Egypt.'"[21]	בְּצֵאתִי מִמִּצְרָיִם:

You might suppose	**יָכוֹל**
that we ought to begin on *Rosh Chodesh*,[22]	מֵרֹאשׁ חֹדֶשׁ,
however, we are taught, "On that day."[23]	תַּלְמוּד לוֹמַר בַּיּוֹם הַהוּא.
If the interpretation is based "On that day,"	אִי בַּיּוֹם הַהוּא,
you might assume	יָכוֹל
that it means during the daytime,	מִבְּעוֹד יוֹם.
however, we are taught, "Because of this."[24]	תַּלְמוּד לוֹמַר, בַּעֲבוּר זֶה.
I would not have quoted, "Because of this"	בַּעֲבוּר זֶה לֹא אָמַרְתִּי

---

[20] Since his question is so simple, he should be answered without any complicated explanations. It is sufficient merely to quote the Biblical verse, *Shemos* 13:8.

[21] *Shemos* 13:5.

[22] We might suppose that the recital of the Haggadah takes place on *Rosh Chodesh*, the first day of the month of *Nissan*, as is stated "וְעָבַדְתָּ אֶת הָעֲבוֹדָה הַזֹּאת בַּחֹדֶשׁ הַזֶּה, You shall do this service in this month (of Nissan)" (*Shemos* 13:8).

[23] The Torah teaches us "וְהִגַּדְתָּ לְבִנְךָ בַּיּוֹם הַהוּא, You shall tell your son the story *on that day*," meaning the day when Pesach is actually celebrated.

[24] The last words of the above verse states, "בַּעֲבוּר זֶה עָשָׂה ה' לִי בְּצֵאתִי מִמִּצְרָיִם, Because of this did Adonoy do for me when I went out of Egypt."

except to stipulate that this clearly means	אֶלָּא
that the Haggadah is to be said only at a time	בְּשָׁעָה
when both *matzoh* and *marror*	שֶׁיֵּשׁ מַצָּה וּמָרוֹר,
are set before you.	מֻנָּחִים לְפָנֶיךָ:

Originally מִתְּחִלָּה

our ancestors were idol worshippers,	עוֹבְדֵי כוֹכָבִים הָיוּ אֲבוֹתֵינוּ.
but now	וְעַכְשָׁו
God[25] has drawn us close to serve Him,	קֵרְבָנוּ הַמָּקוֹם לַעֲבוֹדָתוֹ.
as it is said,	שֶׁנֶּאֱמַר:
"And Yehoshua spoke to all the people saying,	וַיֹּאמֶר יְהוֹשֻׁעַ אֶל־כָּל־הָעָם.
'Thus spoke Adonoy, God of Israel:	כֹּה אָמַר יְיָ אֱלֹהֵי יִשְׂרָאֵל,
'From beyond the [Euphrates] river[26]	בְּעֵבֶר הַנָּהָר
did your ancestors originate,	יָשְׁבוּ אֲבוֹתֵיכֶם מֵעוֹלָם,
[that is] Terach,	תֶּרַח
father of Avrohom and Nachor.[27]	אֲבִי אַבְרָהָם וַאֲבִי נָחוֹר.
They served other gods.	וַיַּעַבְדוּ אֱלֹהִים אֲחֵרִים:
But I took your father Avrohom	וָאֶקַּח אֶת־אֲבִיכֶם אֶת־אַבְרָהָם
from beyond the [Euphrates] river[26]	מֵעֵבֶר הַנָּהָר,
and led him throughout the land of Canaan.	וָאוֹלֵךְ אוֹתוֹ בְּכָל־אֶרֶץ כְּנָעַן.
I multiplied his descendants	וָאַרְבֶּה אֶת־זַרְעוֹ,
and gave him [a son] Yitzchok,	וָאֶתֶּן־לוֹ אֶת־יִצְחָק:

[25] This reference to God, *ha-makom*, literally means "the place", implying that God is everywhere, the Ruler of the whole world. Thus, the name *makom* indicates that He is the place of the world, but the world is not His sole place.

[26] The name *Ivrim* (Hebrews) is derived from the fact that Avrohom came from beyond (mei eiver) the river. Why is this phrase stressed by being repeated twice? To emphasize that the whole world was on one side [worshipping idols] and Avrohom was on the other side [serving God].

[27] Nachor is mentioned to show that Avrohom the other son of Terach, could easily have been forgotten like his brother Nachor—forgotten by history. Instead Avrohom became the father of the Jewish People.

and to Yitzchok I gave [two sons]	וָאֶתֵּן לְיִצְחָק
Yaakov and Eisav.	אֶת־יַעֲקֹב וְאֶת־עֵשָׂו.
To Eisav, I gave Mount Seir[28]	וָאֶתֵּן לְעֵשָׂו אֶת־הַר שֵׂעִיר,
as his inheritance,	לָרֶשֶׁת אוֹתוֹ.
but Yaakov and his sons went down to Egypt.	וְיַעֲקֹב וּבָנָיו יָרְדוּ מִצְרָיִם:

Blessed is He	בָּרוּךְ
Who keeps His promise to Israel,	שׁוֹמֵר הַבְטָחָתוֹ לְיִשְׂרָאֵל.
blessed is He;	בָּרוּךְ הוּא.
for the Holy One blessed is He	שֶׁהַקָּדוֹשׁ בָּרוּךְ הוּא
pre-determined the end of our bondage	חִשַּׁב אֶת־הַקֵּץ לַעֲשׂוֹת,
in fulfillment of what He said	כְּמָה שֶׁאָמַר
to our father, Avrohom,	לְאַבְרָהָם אָבִינוּ
at the covenant of the pieces,	בִּבְרִית בֵּין הַבְּתָרִים.
as it is said (*Bereishis* 15:13,14):	שֶׁנֶּאֱמַר:
And He said to Avram:	וַיֹּאמֶר לְאַבְרָם,
"Know for sure	יָדֹעַ תֵּדַע,
that your descendants will be foreigners	כִּי־גֵר יִהְיֶה זַרְעֲךָ,
in a land that is not theirs.	בְּאֶרֶץ לֹא לָהֶם,
They will enslave them and oppress them	וַעֲבָדוּם וְעִנּוּ אֹתָם.
[for] four hundred years.	אַרְבַּע מֵאוֹת שָׁנָה:

---

[28] Here we see a contrast between Eisav and Yaakov. While Eisav's descendants went up to claim Mount Seir as their inheritance, Yaakov's children were going down to Egypt. Before the Bnei Yisroel could claim their inheritance, they had to experience slavery in Egypt. They learned how to treat the stranger, the homeless and the poor—"כִּי גֵרִים הֱיִיתֶם בְּאֶרֶץ מִצְרָיִם—because you were strangers in the land of Egypt." By contrast, Eisav's offspring first went to Seir and became established in their land. When the Bnei Yisroel, their cousins, tried to pass through their land after wandering in the desert, the children of Eisav refused to allow them passage or provisions. Eisav's offspring were no longer the descendants of an Avrohom, who provided the traveler with hospitality (*Metsudas Avrohom*).

But also that nation whom they will serve	וְגַם אֶת־הַגּוֹי אֲשֶׁר יַעֲבֹדוּ,
I will judge;	דָּן אָנֹכִי.
afterwards they will leave with great wealth.	וְאַחֲרֵי־כֵן יֵצְאוּ, בִּרְכֻשׁ גָּדוֹל:

The cup of wine is raised.

Here the cup of wine is raised in thanksgiving, and as a re-affirmation of our faith in our ultimate redemption. The matzos remain covered.

It is that [pledge to Avrohom, our father]	**וְהִיא**
that has sustained our forefathers and us,	שֶׁעָמְדָה לַאֲבוֹתֵינוּ וְלָנוּ.
for it has not been merely one [ruler or nation]	שֶׁלֹּא אֶחָד בִּלְבָד,
who has arisen, determined to destroy us.	עָמַד עָלֵינוּ לְכַלּוֹתֵנוּ.
Rather, in every generation	אֶלָּא שֶׁבְּכָל דּוֹר וָדוֹר,
there arises those who would destroy us.	עוֹמְדִים עָלֵינוּ לְכַלּוֹתֵנוּ.
But the Holy One, blessed is He,	וְהַקָּדוֹשׁ בָּרוּךְ הוּא
has always rescued us from their hands.[29]	מַצִּילֵנוּ מִיָּדָם:

The cup of wine is set down, and the matzos are uncovered.

Consider and learn	**צֵא** וּלְמַד,
what Lavan, the Aramean, intended[30]	מַה בִּקֵּשׁ לָבָן הָאֲרַמִּי:

---

[29] Our deliverance never came about through natural or normal events, but only through the miraculous intervention of the Rebono shel Olam (*Metsudas Avrohom*).

[30] The Haggadah teaches us that in every generation there are those who rise up against us, even though we are often unaware of their evil intentions. This we can learn from Lavan, whose intention to harm Yaakov was certainly not obvious, when he pretended to be hurt at being denied the opportunity of bidding farewell to his daughters and grandchildren. Yet the Torah bears witness that his intention was to destroy the family of Yaakov and thus jeapordize the destiny of Israel (*Vilna Gaon*).

to do to our father, Yaakov.	לַעֲשׂוֹת לְיַעֲקֹב אָבִינוּ.
Pharaoh issued his decree of extermination	שֶׁפַּרְעֹה לֹא גָזַר
only against the newborn males	אֶלָּא עַל־הַזְּכָרִים.
whereas Lavan sought to exterminate everyone,	וְלָבָן בִּקֵּשׁ לַעֲקֹר אֶת־הַכֹּל.
as it is said (*Devorim* 26:5),	שֶׁנֶּאֱמַר:
An Aramean	אֲרַמִּי
intended to destroy my father (Yaakov)[31]	אֹבֵד אָבִי,
but he went down to Egypt,[32]	וַיֵּרֶד מִצְרַיְמָה,
and he sojourned there	וַיָּגָר שָׁם
with his family few in number[33]	בִּמְתֵי מְעָט.
but there he became a nation	וַיְהִי־שָׁם לְגוֹי
great, mighty and numerous.	גָּדוֹל, עָצוּם וָרָב:
"He went down to Egypt"—	וַיֵּרֶד מִצְרַיְמָה.
impelled by the Divine Decree.[34]	אָנוּס עַל פִּי הַדִּבּוּר.
"And he sojourned there"—	וַיָּגָר שָׁם.
this teaches us	מְלַמֵּד

---

[31] Because Lavan *intended* to destroy Yaakov, the Almighty accounted it to him as though he had *actually* done so, for concerning the nations of the world, the Holy One, Blessed is He, accounts their intention as an actual deed (*Rashi* from *Sifri*).

[32] There were others, too, who wanted to harm us, for afterwards Yaakov went down to Egypt [with his children and they were enslaved there] (*Rashi*). This statement is not a continuation of the previous one, for Yaakov did not go down to Egypt as a consequence of Lavan's attempt to destroy him. He who brings Bikurim, the first fruit, merely tells of another similar attempt to harm us and a second instance of God's lovingkindness.

[33] He went down with his family of seventy souls.

[34] This was the beginning of what the Almighty foretold to Avraham: יָדֹעַ תֵּדַע כִּי גֵר יִהְיֶה זַרְעֲךָ בְּאֶרֶץ לֹא לָהֶם וַעֲבָדוּם וְעִנּוּ אֹתָם אַרְבַּע מֵאוֹת שָׁנָה, "Know for sure that your descendants will be strangers, foreigners in a land that is not theirs, they will enslave and oppress them for four hundred years."

that our father Yaakov did not intend	שֶׁלֹּא יָרַד יַעֲקֹב אָבִינוּ
to settle permanently in Egypt,	לְהִשְׁתַּקֵּעַ בְּמִצְרַיִם.
rather to reside there as a sojourner	אֶלָּא לָגוּר שָׁם.
as it is said (*Bereishis* 47:4).	שֶׁנֶּאֱמַר:
"They [Yaakov's sons] said to Pharaoh;	וַיֹּאמְרוּ אֶל־פַּרְעֹה,
'We have come to live in the land temporarily	לָגוּר בָּאָרֶץ בָּאנוּ,
since there is no pasture	כִּי־אֵין מִרְעֶה
for your servant's flocks;	לַצֹּאן אֲשֶׁר לַעֲבָדֶיךָ,
because the famine is severe in Canaan.	כִּי־כָבֵד הָרָעָב בְּאֶרֶץ כְּנָעַן
Now then, please let your servants live	וְעַתָּה, יֵשְׁבוּ־נָא עֲבָדֶיךָ
in the land of Goshen."	בְּאֶרֶץ גֹּשֶׁן:

"Few in number," as it is said, (*Devorim* 10:22)	בִּמְתֵי מְעָט. כְּמָה שֶׁנֶּאֱמַר:
"With [a mere] seventy persons	בְּשִׁבְעִים נֶפֶשׁ,
did your forefathers go down to Egypt;	יָרְדוּ אֲבֹתֶיךָ מִצְרָיְמָה.
and now Adonoy, your God has made you	וְעַתָּה, שָׂמְךָ יְיָ אֱלֹהֶיךָ,
as numerous as the stars of heaven.	כְּכוֹכְבֵי הַשָּׁמַיִם לָרֹב:

"And there he became a nation"—	וַיְהִי שָׁם לְגוֹי.
which teaches us	מְלַמֵּד
that the Jews were distinctive there.[35]	שֶׁהָיוּ יִשְׂרָאֵל מְצֻיָּנִים שָׁם:

"Great, mighty"	גָּדוֹל עָצוּם.
as it is said (*Shemos* 2:7)	כְּמָה שֶׁנֶּאֱמַר:
"And the B'nei Yisroel were fertile and prolific,	וּבְנֵי יִשְׂרָאֵל, פָּרוּ וַיִּשְׁרְצוּ,

[35] This teaches that the Jews distinguished themselves in Egypt. They became unique through their traditions so that were recognized and acknowledged as a separate nation. They were not suspected of sexual immorality or of slander, and they did not change their names or language or attire to conform to Egyptian culture (*Mechilta*).

and they multiplied	וַיִּרְבּוּ
and became very, very mighty;[36]	וַיַּעַצְמוּ, בִּמְאֹד מְאֹד.
and the land was filled with them."	וַתִּמָּלֵא הָאָרֶץ אֹתָם:
"And numerous," as it is said (Yechezkiel 16:7):	וָרָב. כְּמָה שֶׁנֶּאֱמַר:
"I caused you to thrive	רְבָבָה
as the plant of the field,[37]	כְּצֶמַח הַשָּׂדֶה נְתַתִּיךְ,
and you grew and developed	וַתִּרְבִּי, וַתִּגְדְּלִי,
and you attained great charm;	וַתָּבֹאִי בַּעֲדִי עֲדָיִים.
[you were] beautiful of figure	שָׁדַיִם נָכֹנוּ,
and your hair amply grown;	וּשְׂעָרֵךְ צִמֵּחַ,
but you were [still] naked and bare.	וְאַתְּ עֵרֹם וְעֶרְיָה:
And I passed over you	וָאֶעֱבֹר עָלַיִךְ
and I saw you wallowing in your blood,	וָאֶרְאֵךְ מִתְבּוֹסֶסֶת בְּדָמָיִךְ,
and I said to you,	וָאֹמַר לָךְ,
'Through your blood you shall live,'	בְּדָמַיִךְ חֲיִי,
and I said to you,	וָאֹמַר לָךְ,
'Through your blood you shall live.'"[38]	בְּדָמַיִךְ חֲיִי:

[36] Even though in the case of multiple births, it is common that the infants are less sturdy than a baby born in a single birth, nevertheless, when the Jewish mothers in Egypt gave birth to six babies at a time, they were not only numerous, but mighty (Zevach Pesach).

[37] It is the nature of grass that the more it is cut, the more it grows. The Bnei Yisroel were thus compared to the "plants of the field" (grass). The more they were afflicted by the Egyptians, the more they multiplied and flourished (Avudraham).

[38] These two verses selected by the Haggadah are taken from the Prophet Yechezkiel, who in parable fashion, describes Israel's life in Egypt and its redemption. In verses 4–6 he depicts Israel as an infant girl, abandoned at birth. She lies in an open field, filthy and neglected, wallowing in her blood, with no one to show her compassion. Instead of being repulsed by her condition, she (Israel) is promised she will live through her blood, which our Sages interpret as referring to the blood of the Pesach offering and the blood of the circumcision. The prophet describes her (Israel) as naked and bare, which the Sifri renders: naked and bare of mitzvos. In order to be worthy of redemption from Pharaoh's slavery, the Jews had to show themselves willing to become slaves to the Almighty. The fulfillment of the mitzvos of Korbon Pesach and circumcision would express their willingness to do so (Lekutei Avrohom).

The Egyptians did evil to us
and they oppressed us
and imposed hard labor upon us (*Devorim* 26:6).

וַיָּרֵעוּ אֹתָנוּ הַמִּצְרִים
וַיְעַנּוּנוּ.
וַיִּתְּנוּ עָלֵינוּ עֲבֹדָה קָשָׁה:

"The Egyptians did evil[39] to us,"
as it is said, (*Shemos* 1:10)
"Come let us deal wisely with them
lest they increase so much
that should there be a war,
they will join our enemies
and fight against us,
driving us from the land."

וַיָּרֵעוּ אֹתָנוּ הַמִּצְרִים,
כְּמָה שֶׁנֶּאֱמַר:
הָבָה נִתְחַכְּמָה לוֹ.
פֶּן־יִרְבֶּה
וְהָיָה כִּי־תִקְרֶאנָה מִלְחָמָה,
וְנוֹסַף גַּם־הוּא עַל־שֹׂנְאֵינוּ,
וְנִלְחַם־בָּנוּ
וְעָלָה מִן־הָאָרֶץ:

"And afflicted us," as it is said, (*Shemos* 1:11)
"They appointed taskmasters over them
to oppress them
by making them do these hard labors.[40]
They built supply cities for Pharaoh,
Pisom and Ramseis.[41]

וַיְעַנּוּנוּ. כְּמָה שֶׁנֶּאֱמַר:
וַיָּשִׂימוּ עָלָיו שָׂרֵי מִסִּים
לְמַעַן עַנֹּתוֹ
בְּסִבְלֹתָם:
וַיִּבֶן עָרֵי מִסְכְּנוֹת לְפַרְעֹה,
אֶת־פִּתֹם וְאֶת־רַעַמְסֵס:

"And imposed hard labor upon us,
as it is said, (*Shemos* 1:13)
"The Egyptians enslaved the Bnei Yisroel
with body breaking labor.[42]

וַיִּתְּנוּ עָלֵינוּ עֲבֹדָה קָשָׁה.
כְּמָה שֶׁנֶּאֱמַר:
וַיַּעֲבִדוּ מִצְרַיִם אֶת־בְּנֵי יִשְׂרָאֵל
בְּפָרֶךְ:

[39] The word וַיָּרֵעוּ can also be taken literally to mean, "and they made us look bad." Before then, remembering Yoseph with favor, the average Egyptian was friendly and even grateful to the Jews. Therefore, Pharaoh's plan was to inspire fear and envy of the Jews. He began by depicting them as potentially dangerous enemies.

[40] Pharaoh then conscripted the Jews to do hard labor, which he could rationalize as a reasonable demand on foreign immigrants in the land.

[41] These cities were built on marshy, water logged ground, and thus, the walls built by the Jews promptly collapsed or sank into the marshes. As a result, they had to start the entire process over again (*Malbim*).

[42] The Sages comment that the word בְּפָרֶךְ can also mean, "with a soft [smooth] tongue בְּפֶה־רַךְ. Pharaoh proclaimed: "Do me a favor and come work with me." Seeing Pharaoh

We cried out to Adonoy וַנִּצְעַק אֶל־יְיָ

the God of our fathers אֱלֹהֵי אֲבֹתֵינוּ,

and Adonoy heard our plea וַיִּשְׁמַע יְיָ אֶת־קֹלֵנוּ,

and saw our affliction, our burden וַיַּרְא אֶת־עָנְיֵנוּ, וְאֶת־עֲמָלֵנוּ,

and our oppression (*Devarim* 26:7). וְאֶת־לַחֲצֵנוּ:

"We cried out to Adonoy, the God of our fathers" וַנִּצְעַק אֶל־יְיָ אֱלֹהֵי אֲבוֹתֵינוּ.

as it is said, (*Shemos* 2:23): כְּמָה שֶׁנֶּאֱמַר:

"A long time passed וַיְהִי בַיָּמִים הָרַבִּים הָהֵם,

and the king of Egypt died. וַיָּמָת מֶלֶךְ מִצְרַיִם,

The Bnei Yisroel moaned וַיֵּאָנְחוּ בְנֵי־יִשְׂרָאֵל

because of their enslavement, and they cried.[43] מִן־הָעֲבֹדָה וַיִּזְעָקוּ,

Their plea ascended to God וַתַּעַל שַׁוְעָתָם אֶל־הָאֱלֹהִים

because of their bondage."[44] מִן־הָעֲבֹדָה:

"And Adonoy heard our plea," וַיִּשְׁמַע יְיָ אֶת־קוֹלֵנוּ.

as it is said, (*Shemos* 2:24): כְּמָה שֶׁנֶּאֱמַר:

"God heard their groaning[45] וַיִּשְׁמַע אֱלֹהִים אֶת־נַאֲקָתָם.

working, the Jews joined in, and worked diligently all day long. At dusk, taskmasters appeared, who counted the number of bricks each had made. Pharaoh then said, "Now you must work to fulfill the same quota every day, for you are my slaves" (*Lekutei Avrohom*).

[43] Why is the crying out linked with the death of Pharaoh? With the death of the Pharaoh, who had instituted the slavery and persecution, the Jews hoped for the revocation or lapse of the harsh decrees. When the new Pharaoh renewed the decrees, they realized the persecution was not just the whim of one ruler, but a matter of Egyptian policy. The Jews felt the hoplessness of their plight and cried out to God (*Malbim*).

Under the pretense of mourning over Pharaoh's death, the Bnei Yisroel cried out because of their bitter enslavement (*Sheloh*).

[44] If there was a shortage of building materials, the Egyptian taskmasters would entomb the Jews, alive, in the walls of the buildings. The Jews cried out from the walls. God heard their cry.

[45] See *Shemos* 3:7,8. "Adonoy said, 'I have indeed seen the suffering of My people that are in Egypt. I have heard their cry because of their taskmasters, and I am mindful of their pain. I have descended to free them from the hand of Egypt and to bring them up from that land, etc."

and God remembered His covenant[46]	וַיִּזְכֹּר אֱלֹהִים אֶת־בְּרִיתוֹ,
with Avraham, with Yitzchok	אֶת־אַבְרָהָם, אֶת־יִצְחָק
and with Yaakov."	וְאֶת־יַעֲקֹב:
"And saw our affliction,"	וַיַּרְא אֶת־עָנְיֵנוּ.
this refers to the enforced separation	זוֹ פְּרִישׁוּת
of husbands and wives,[47]	דֶּרֶךְ אֶרֶץ.
as it is said, (Shemos 2:25):	כְּמָה שֶׁנֶּאֱמַר:
"And God noted [the plight] of the Bnei Yisroel	וַיַּרְא אֱלֹהִים אֶת־בְּנֵי יִשְׂרָאֵל.
and God knew.[48]	וַיֵּדַע אֱלֹהִים:
"Our burden"	וְאֶת־עֲמָלֵנוּ.
this refers to the children	אֵלּוּ הַבָּנִים.
as it is said, (Shemos 1:22):	כְּמָה שֶׁנֶּאֱמַר:
"Every boy that is born	כָּל־הַבֵּן הַיִּלּוֹד
must be thrown into the river,[49]	הַיְאֹרָה תַּשְׁלִיכֻהוּ,
but every girl shall be allowed to live."[50]	וְכָל־הַבַּת תְּחַיּוּן:

[46] Even though the zchus Avos (merit of the Patriarchs) might no longer be effective, the Bris Avos, (the covenant of the Patriarchs) is always effective (Rabbeinu Tam, Tosfos, Masechet Shabbos 55a).

[47] The Egyptians decreed that the men must sleep in the fields and the women in the cities in order to decrease their offspring. But the Jewish women would cook food and bring it to their husbands. They would comfort their husbands by saying, "We will not be enslaved forever; the Holy One will redeem us." They then would come together and have children. Thus said our Sages, "Our ancestors were redeemed from Egypt, due to the merit of the righteous women in that generation."

[48] The word וַיֵּדַע, and He knew, is often used in the Torah as a euphemism for marital relations.

[49] This reveals that the true intent of the Egyptians was the total destruction of the Jews, not their enslavement. If the Egyptians wanted slaves, they would not have killed the children and so decrease the potential slave population. The slavery was a slow, calculated means of killing the Jews, rather than a source of cheap labor (Metsudes Avrohom).

[50] Why did Pharaoh let the girls live? His plan was to kill all the male children and force the females to marry Egyptians. This was a terrible torture for parents, who knew what would happen to their daughters, as they reached maturity and would be forced to live with the murderers of their people (Haggadah K'Pshutah).

"And our oppression"	וְאֶת־לַחֲצֵנוּ.
this means crushing repression	זוֹ הַדְּחַק,
as it is said, (Shemos 3:9):	כְּמָה שֶׁנֶּאֱמַר:
"I have also seen the oppression	וְגַם־רָאִיתִי אֶת־הַלַּחַץ,
with which the Egyptians oppress them."	אֲשֶׁר מִצְרַיִם לֹחֲצִים אֹתָם:
Adonoy brought us out of Egypt	**וַיּוֹצִאֵנוּ** יְיָ מִמִּצְרַיִם,
with a mighty hand, with an outstretched arm,	בְּיָד חֲזָקָה, וּבִזְרֹעַ נְטוּיָה,
with awesome power,	וּבְמֹרָא גָּדֹל.
with signs and with wonders (Devorim 26:8).	וּבְאֹתוֹת וּבְמֹפְתִים:
"Adonoy brought us out of Egypt"—	וַיּוֹצִיאֵנוּ יְיָ מִמִּצְרַיִם.
not through an angel,	לֹא עַל־יְדֵי מַלְאָךְ,
not through a seraph,	וְלֹא עַל־יְדֵי שָׂרָף,
not through a messenger.	וְלֹא עַל־יְדֵי שָׁלִיחַ.
Rather, the Holy One, blessed is He,	אֶלָּא הַקָּדוֹשׁ בָּרוּךְ הוּא
in His glory, He, Himself,	בִּכְבוֹדוֹ וּבְעַצְמוֹ.
as it is said, (Shemos 12:12):	שֶׁנֶּאֱמַר:
"I will pass through the land of Egypt[51]	וְעָבַרְתִּי בְאֶרֶץ־מִצְרַיִם
on that night,	בַּלַּיְלָה הַזֶּה.
and I will strike [kill] every firstborn	וְהִכֵּיתִי כָל־בְּכוֹר
in the land of Egypt[52]	בְּאֶרֶץ מִצְרַיִם

[51] Rashi, quoting the Mechilta, states that וְעָבַרְתִּי (I will pass through) should not be taken literally, but rather as a term used to describe a king passing from place to place in his country. It is used here as a metaphor describing God's activity. He adds that the comparison extends only to the idea of an earthly king passing through his dominion to judge and punish. Such a king must pass from place to place, judging his subjects. He cannot do so simultaneously, but only when he arrives at the place of their abode. God, however, who is not subject to limitations of time and space, slew all the firstborn at the same moment.

[52] The words בְּאֶרֶץ מִצְרַיִם appear unnecessary since they were used immediately before in this verse. They are used again to stress that every firstborn in the land of Egypt, even the firstborn of other nations who happened to be in Egypt would be slain. Also the firstborn of the Egyptians who happened to be in other countries would be slain (Rashi).

both man and beast	מֵאָדָם וְעַד־בְּהֵמָה,
and against all the gods of Egypt[53]	וּבְכָל־אֱלֹהֵי מִצְרַיִם,
I will execute judgements; I am Adonoy."	אֶעֱשֶׂה שְׁפָטִים, אֲנִי יְיָ.

"I will pass through the land of Egypt	וְעָבַרְתִּי בְאֶרֶץ־מִצְרַיִם
on that night—"	בַּלַּיְלָה הַזֶּה,
I and not an angel.[54]	אֲנִי וְלֹא מַלְאָךְ.
"I will strike every firstborn	וְהִכֵּיתִי כָל־בְּכוֹר
in the land of Egypt"—	בְּאֶרֶץ מִצְרַיִם,
I and not a seraph.	אֲנִי וְלֹא שָׂרָף.
"Against all the gods of Egypt	וּבְכָל־אֱלֹהֵי מִצְרַיִם
I will execute judgements"—	אֶעֱשֶׂה שְׁפָטִים,
I and not a messenger.[55]	אֲנִי וְלֹא הַשָּׁלִיחַ.
"I am Adonoy" I and no other.	אֲנִי יְיָ, אֲנִי הוּא וְלֹא אַחֵר:

"With a mighty hand."	בְּיָד חֲזָקָה.
This refers to pestilence,	זוֹ הַדֶּבֶר.
as it is said, (*Shemos* 9:3):	כְּמָה שֶׁנֶּאֱמַר:
"Behold, the hand of Adonoy	הִנֵּה יַד־יְיָ
is directed at your livestock in the field—	הוֹיָה בְּמִקְנְךָ אֲשֶׁר בַּשָּׂדֶה,
the horses, the donkeys	בַּסּוּסִים בַּחֲמֹרִים
the camels, the cattle and the sheep—	בַּגְּמַלִּים, בַּבָּקָר וּבַצֹּאן.

[53] An idol of wood rotted, and one of metal melted and was poured out on the ground (*Rashi* from *Mechilta*).

[54] This refers to the Angel of Death who was not permitted to perform his function on that night. On a usual night he would have taken the lives of a number of victims who would have normally been called to death among the large Jewish population. If any of them would have died that night, the Egyptians would have been able to claim that the Jews were also included in the slaying of the firstborn. Thus, the Angel of Death was forbidden to slay even those Jews who would have died a natural death (*Vilna Gaon*).

[55] This might have referred to Moshe, who was God's select messenger, and whose name is not mentioned in the entire Haggadah (*Lekutei Avraham*).

there will be a very serious pestilence."   דֶּבֶר כָּבֵד מְאֹד:

"With an outstretched arm."   וּבִזְרֹעַ נְטוּיָה

This refers to the sword   זוֹ הַחֶרֶב.

as it is said, (*I Divrei Hayomim* 2:16):   כְּמָה שֶׁנֶּאֱמַר:

"And His unsheathed sword in His hand   וְחַרְבּוֹ שְׁלוּפָה בְּיָדוֹ,

outstretched against Jerusalem."[56]   נְטוּיָה עַל־יְרוּשָׁלָםִ:

"With awesome power."   וּבְמֹרָא גָדוֹל.

This refers to   זוֹ

the Revelation of the Divine Presence,   גִּלּוּי שְׁכִינָה.

as it is said, (*Devorim* 4:34):   כְּמָה שֶׁנֶּאֱמַר:

"Has God ever ventured   אוֹ הֲנִסָּה אֱלֹהִים,

to go and take for Himself   לָבוֹא לָקַחַת לוֹ

one nation from the midst of another   גוֹי מִקֶּרֶב גּוֹי,

by trials, by signs, and wondrous deeds,   בְּמַסֹּת בְּאֹתֹת וּבְמוֹפְתִים

by battle, with a mighty hand,   וּבְמִלְחָמָה, וּבְיָד חֲזָקָה

with an outstretched arm,   וּבִזְרוֹעַ נְטוּיָה,

and with awesome power   וּבְמוֹרָאִים גְּדֹלִים.

as all that was done for you   כְּכֹל אֲשֶׁר־עָשָׂה לָכֶם,

by Adonoy, your God,   יְיָ אֱלֹהֵיכֶם,

in Egypt, before your eyes."   בְּמִצְרַיִם לְעֵינֶיךָ:

"With signs" refers to the staff [of Moshe]   וּבְאֹתוֹת. זֶה הַמַּטֶּה.

as it is said, (*Shemos* 4:17):   כְּמָה שֶׁנֶּאֱמַר:

"Take this staff in your hand[57]   וְאֶת־הַמַּטֶּה הַזֶּה, תִּקַּח בְּיָדֶךָ.

for with it you shall perform   אֲשֶׁר תַּעֲשֶׂה־בּוֹ

the miraculous signs."   אֶת־הָאֹתֹת:

---

[56] The verse couples the words חַרְבּוֹ שְׁלוּפָה (unsheathed sword) with זְרֹעַ נְטוּיָה (outstretched hand).

[57] This staff was given to Moshe when God revealed Himself to him at the burning bush, where Moshe accepted his mission to go to Egypt (*Ritvah*).

"With wonders" refers to the blood	וּבְמֹפְתִים. זֶה הַדָּם.
as it is said, (*Yoeil* 3:3):	כְּמָה שֶׁנֶּאֱמַר:
"I will show wonders	וְנָתַתִּי מוֹפְתִים,
in the sky and on the earth,	בַּשָּׁמַיִם וּבָאָרֶץ.
BLOOD and FIRE	דָּם. וָאֵשׁ.
and COLUMNS OF SMOKE.[58]	וְתִימְרוֹת עָשָׁן:

Spill three drops of wine, one at the mention of each word[59]

Another explanation	דָּבָר אַחֵר.
[of the verse quoted from *Devorim* 26:8.	
See page 27.]	

This explanation, establishes that the total number of plagues add up to ten; by counting each of the first three two-word phrases and the plural forms of the last two words, as follows.

With a *mighty hand,* indicates two,	בְּיָד חֲזָקָה שְׁתַּיִם.
and with an *outstretched arm,* indicates two,	וּבִזְרֹעַ נְטוּיָה שְׁתַּיִם.
and with *awesome power,* indicates two,	וּבְמֹרָא גָּדֹל שְׁתַּיִם.
with *signs,* indicates two,	וּבְאֹתוֹת שְׁתַּיִם.
and with *wonders,* indicates two.	וּבְמֹפְתִים שְׁתַּיִם:
These are the ten plagues	אֵלּוּ עֶשֶׂר מַכּוֹת
that the Holy One Blessed is He, inflicted	שֶׁהֵבִיא הַקָּדוֹשׁ בָּרוּךְ הוּא

---

[58] This verse actually refers to the Messianic redemption rather than of the Exodus from Egypt. It is quoted in the Haggadah to indicate that the word מוֹפֵת, (wonders) refers to blood.

[59] The most common explanation of this custom is that it shows that even as we rejoice over the downfall of our enemies, we remember that they, too, are human, and so we rejoice with less than a full heart (or a full cup).

upon the Egyptians in Egypt,	עַל־הַמִּצְרִים בְּמִצְרָיִם.
They are:	וְאֵלוּ הֵן:

At each mention of a plague and again at each of the terms used by Rabbi Yehudah, a drop of wine is spilled. The cup must be refilled afterwards.

BLOOD, FROGS, LICE, BEASTS,	דָּם. צְפַרְדֵּעַ. כִּנִּים. עָרוֹב.
PESTILENCE, BOILS, HAIL, LOCUSTS,	דֶּבֶר. שְׁחִין. בָּרָד. אַרְבֶּה.
DARKNESS, SLAYING OF THE FIRSTBORN.	חֹשֶׁךְ. מַכַּת בְּכוֹרוֹת:

Rabbi Yehudah	רַבִּי יְהוּדָה
made an acrostic of the plagues.[60]	הָיָה נוֹתֵן בָּהֶם סִמָּנִים:

D'TSACH,	ADASH	B'AHCHAV	דְּצַ"ךְ	עַדַ"שׁ	בְּאַחַ"ב
D–Dom	A–Arov	B–Borod	דָּם.	עָרוֹב.	בָּרָד.
TS–TSfardaya	D–Dever	AH–AHrbeh	צְפַרְדֵּעַ.	דֶּבֶר.	אַרְבֶּה.
CH–Kinim	SH–SH'chin	CH–CHoshech	כִּנִּים.	שְׁחִין.	חֹשֶׁךְ.
		V(B)–makas			מַכַּת
		b'choros			בְּכוֹרוֹת:

Rabbi Yose Haglili says:	רַבִּי יוֹסֵי הַגְּלִילִי אוֹמֵר:
How can you deduce the fact	מִנַּיִן אַתָּה אוֹמֵר,
that though the Egyptians were smitten	שֶׁלָּקוּ הַמִּצְרִים
in Egypt	בְּמִצְרַיִם
with [only] ten plagues,	עֶשֶׂר מַכּוֹת,
they were dealt fifty plagues at the [Reed] Sea?	וְעַל־הַיָּם, לָקוּ חֲמִשִּׁים מַכּוֹת

[60] Rabbi Yehudah takes the first Hebrew letter of each plague to form an acrostic. A number of reasons are given for this. He wanted to stress the plagues, using an acrostic as an easy way to remember them and to emphasize them. He also wished to stress the tradition of ten plagues in their specific order as presented in *Seifer Shemos*.

Concerning the plagues *within* Egypt,	בְּמִצְרַיִם
what is stated?	מָה הוּא אוֹמֵר:
"Then the magicians said to Pharaoh,	וַיֹּאמְרוּ הַחַרְטֻמִּם אֶל־פַּרְעֹה,
'It is the finger of God'"(*Shemos* 8:15).[61]	אֶצְבַּע אֱלֹהִים הִוא.
With reference to what happened at the Sea,	וְעַל־הַיָּם
what is stated?	מָה הוּא אוֹמֵר:
"And Israel saw the great hand[62]	וַיַּרְא יִשְׂרָאֵל אֶת־הַיָּד הַגְּדֹלָה,
which Adonoy wielded against Egypt	אֲשֶׁר עָשָׂה יְיָ בְּמִצְרַיִם,
and the people feared Adonoy	וַיִּירְאוּ הָעָם אֶת־יְיָ.
and they believed in Adonoy	וַיַּאֲמִינוּ בַּיָי,
and that Moshe was His servant" (*Shemos* 14:31).	וּבְמֹשֶׁה עַבְדּוֹ:
How many plagues did they receive	כַּמָּה לָקוּ
by *one finger*?	בָאֶצְבַּע,
Ten plagues!	עֶשֶׂר מַכּוֹת.
From this you may conclude that	אֱמוֹר מֵעַתָּה
whereas in Egypt they received ten plagues,[63]	בְּמִצְרַיִם, לָקוּ עֶשֶׂר מַכּוֹת,
at the Sea they were dealt fifty plagues.[64]	וְעַל־הַיָּם, לָקוּ חֲמִשִּׁים מַכּוֹת:

Rabbi Eliezer says:	רַבִּי אֱלִיעֶזֶר אוֹמֵר:
How can you deduce that each plague	מִנַּיִן שֶׁכָּל־מַכָּה וּמַכָּה,
that the Holy One, Blessed is He, brought	שֶׁהֵבִיא הַקָּדוֹשׁ בָּרוּךְ הוּא
upon the Egyptians within Egypt [proper]	עַל־הַמִּצְרִים בְּמִצְרַיִם,
was the equivalent of four plagues?	הָיְתָה שֶׁל אַרְבַּע מַכּוֹת

[61] This plague (כִּנִּים, lice) is not caused by sorcery; it is of the Divine intervention of God (*Rashi* from *Shemos Rabbah*). Even though this was said at the plague of lice, nevertheless, it applied to all the plagues because the magicians no longer attempted to duplicate any of the plagues (*Ritvah*).

[62] The great hand denotes the *great power* which the *hand* of the Holy, Blessed is He, had exercised against the Egyptians (*Rashi*).

[63] Which were brought on them by one finger of God.

[64] Five times as many by His whole hand—5 fingers! (5 times ten = 50).

	שֶׁנֶּאֱמַר:

As it is said, (*Tehillim* 78:49):

"He cast upon them blazing anger יְשַׁלַּח־בָּם חֲרוֹן אַפּוֹ,

fury, rage and distress, עֶבְרָה וָזַעַם וְצָרָה.

a deputation of angels on a mission of evil." מִשְׁלַחַת מַלְאֲכֵי רָעִים.

FURY, indicates one; RAGE, indicates two; עֶבְרָה אַחַת. וָזַעַם שְׁתַּיִם.

DISTRESS, indicates three; וְצָרָה שָׁלֹשׁ.

a DEPUTATION OF ANGELS on a MISSION מִשְׁלַחַת מַלְאֲכֵי

OF EVIL, four. רָעִים אַרְבַּע.

From this you deduce אֱמוֹר מֵעַתָּה:

that if within Egypt בְּמִצְרַיִם,

they were dealt forty plagues,[65] לָקוּ אַרְבָּעִים מַכּוֹת,

at the Sea, וְעַל־הַיָּם,

they were dealt two hundred plagues.[66] לָקוּ מָאתַיִם מַכּוֹת:

Rabbi Akiva says: רַבִּי עֲקִיבָא אוֹמֵר:

How can you deduce that each plague מִנַּיִן שֶׁכָּל־מַכָּה וּמַכָּה

that the Holy One, Blessed is He, brought שֶׁהֵבִיא הַקָּדוֹשׁ בָּרוּךְ הוּא

upon the Egyptians within Egypt [proper] עַל־הַמִּצְרִים בְּמִצְרַיִם,

was the equivalent of five plagues? הָיְתָה שֶׁל חָמֵשׁ מַכּוֹת?

As it is said, (Ibid.) שֶׁנֶּאֱמַר:

"He cast upon them blazing anger, יְשַׁלַּח־בָּם חֲרוֹן אַפּוֹ

fury, rage and distress, עֶבְרָה וָזַעַם וְצָרָה.

a deputation of angels on a mission of evil." מִשְׁלַחַת מַלְאֲכֵי רָעִים.

BLAZING ANGER, indicates one;[67] חֲרוֹן אַפּוֹ אַחַת.

---

[65] Four times the traditional ten plagues by only *one finger*.

[66] At the sea they were struck by His whole hand, all five fingers, thus five times forty is two hundred.

[67] Rabbi Akiva began enumerating with the very first phrase, not with the second as did Rabbi Eliezer.

FURY, indicates two; RAGE, indicates three; | עֶבְרָה שְׁתַּיִם. וָזַעַם שָׁלֹשׁ.

DISTRESS, indicates four; | וְצָרָה אַרְבַּע.

a DEPUTATION of ANGELS on a MISSION | מִשְׁלַחַת מַלְאֲכֵי

OF EVIL, five. | רָעִים חָמֵשׁ.

From this you deduce | אֱמוֹר מֵעַתָּה:

that if within Egypt they were dealt | בְּמִצְרַיִם, לָקוּ

fifty plagues, | חֲמִשִּׁים מַכּוֹת,

then at the Sea, | וְעַל הַיָּם,

they were dealt two hundred fifty plagues.[68] | לָקוּ חֲמִשִּׁים וּמָאתַיִם מַכּוֹת:

How numerous are the exalted acts | כַּמָּה מַעֲלוֹת טוֹבוֹת

which the All-Present performed for us,[69] | לַמָּקוֹם עָלֵינוּ:

Had He brought us out of Egypt, | אִלּוּ הוֹצִיאָנוּ מִמִּצְרַיִם,

without executing judgments against them,[70] | וְלֹא־עָשָׂה בָהֶם שְׁפָטִים,

it would have been enough for us. | דַּיֵּנוּ:

Had He executed judgments against them | אִלּוּ עָשָׂה בָהֶם שְׁפָטִים,

but not against their gods, | וְלֹא־עָשָׂה בֵאלֹהֵיהֶם,

it would have been enough for us. | דַּיֵּנוּ:

Had He executed judgments against their gods | אִלּוּ עָשָׂה בֵאלֹהֵיהֶם,

but had not slain their firstborn, | וְלֹא־הָרַג אֶת־בְּכוֹרֵיהֶם,

---

[68] Why did the Tanaim Sages find it necessary to define how many plagues the Egyptians were dealt? They wanted to show the full impact of the miracles that accompanied the redemption and exodus from Egypt. In addition, they attempted to project the greatness of God's promise, "Every affliction that I brought upon Egypt, I will not bring upon you" (*Shemos* 15:26). In defining the number of plagues that befell Egypt, they also point out the many afflictions from which the Jewish nation will be spared if it listens and accepts God's words (*Vilna Gaon*).

[69] This listing of God's acts of kindness on our behalf is followed by *Hallel* by which we sing praises to Him. In order to enhance and magnify our praise, the Haggadah portrays in graphic fashion all the great favors God has done for us from the time of the Exodus (*Metsudas Avraham*).

[70] We would have been satisfied had He merely taken us out of bondage, even without having taken revenge against our tormentors (*Zevach Pesach*).

it would have been enough for us.	דַּיֵּנוּ:
Had He slain their firstborn,	אִלּוּ הָרַג אֶת־בְּכוֹרֵיהֶם,
and not given us their wealth,[71]	וְלֹא־נָתַן לָנוּ אֶת־מָמוֹנָם,
it would have been enough for us.	דַּיֵּנוּ:
Had He given us their wealth,	אִלּוּ נָתַן לָנוּ אֶת־מָמוֹנָם,
but had not split the Sea for us,[72]	וְלֹא־קָרַע לָנוּ אֶת־הַיָּם,
it would have been enough for us.	דַּיֵּנוּ:
Had He split the Sea for us,	אִלּוּ קָרַע לָנוּ אֶת־הַיָּם,
without leading us through it on dry land,[73]	וְלֹא־הֶעֱבִירָנוּ בְתוֹכוֹ בֶּחָרָבָה,
it would have been enough for us.	דַּיֵּנוּ:
Had He led us through it on dry land,	אִלּוּ הֶעֱבִירָנוּ בְתוֹכוֹ בֶּחָרָבָה,
without drowning our oppressors in it,[74]	וְלֹא־שִׁקַּע צָרֵינוּ בְּתוֹכוֹ,
it would have been enough for us.	דַּיֵּנוּ:
Had He drowned our oppressors in it	אִלּוּ שִׁקַּע צָרֵינוּ בְּתוֹכוֹ,
without taking care of our needs[75]	וְלֹא־סִפֵּק צָרְכֵּנוּ
in the desert for forty years,	בַּמִּדְבָּר אַרְבָּעִים שָׁנָה,
it would have been enough for us.	דַּיֵּנוּ:
Had He taken care of our needs	אִלּוּ סִפֵּק צָרְכֵּנוּ
in the desert for forty years	בַּמִּדְבָּר אַרְבָּעִים שָׁנָה,

[71] This refers to the wealth the Jews accumulated from the Egyptians after they drowned at the Reed Sea, for otherwise, the wealth that we took from them in Egypt had been promised to Avrohom at the Covenant of the Parts. (See Bereishis 15:14, "Afterwards they will leave with great wealth") (*Rashbam*).

[72] He could have rescued us in a less miraculous fashion (*Rashbam*).

[73] The bottom of the Sea could have been muddy, rather than completely dry and we would have had to slog our way across (*Rashbam*).

[74] He could have returned the Sea to its original form and permitted the Egyptians to return to Egypt (*Rashbam*).

[75] The people had brought along cattle and other livestock from which they could have had provisions. In addition, they had great wealth in silver and gold with which they could have purchased food (*Rashbam*).

without feeding us the *manna*,[76]	וְלֹא־הֶאֱכִילָנוּ אֶת־הַמָּן,
it would have been enough for us.	דַּיֵּנוּ:
Had He fed us the *manna*	אִלּוּ הֶאֱכִילָנוּ אֶת־הַמָּן
without giving us the Shabbos,	וְלֹא־נָתַן לָנוּ אֶת־הַשַּׁבָּת,
it would have been enough for us.	דַּיֵּנוּ:
Had He given us the Shabbos[77]	אִלּוּ נָתַן לָנוּ אֶת הַשַּׁבָּת
without bringing us to Mount Sinai,	וְלֹא קֵרְבָנוּ לִפְנֵי הַר־סִינַי,
it would have been enough for us.	דַּיֵּנוּ:
Had He brought us to Mount Sinai	אִלּוּ קֵרְבָנוּ לִפְנֵי הַר־סִינַי,
without giving us the Torah,[78]	וְלֹא־נָתַן לָנוּ אֶת־הַתּוֹרָה,
it would have been enough for us.	דַּיֵּנוּ:
Had He given us the Torah	אִלּוּ נָתַן לָנוּ אֶת־הַתּוֹרָה,
without bringing us into Eretz Yisroel,	וְלֹא־הִכְנִיסָנוּ לְאֶרֶץ יִשְׂרָאֵל,
it would have been enough for us.	דַּיֵּנוּ:
Had He brought us into Eretz Yisroel	אִלּוּ הִכְנִיסָנוּ לְאֶרֶץ יִשְׂרָאֵל,
without building the Sanctuary for us,	וְלֹא־בָנָה לָנוּ אֶת־בֵּית הַבְּחִירָה,
it would have been enough for us.	דַּיֵּנוּ:

How much more so	עַל אַחַת כַּמָּה וְכַמָּה,
must we multiply our thanks to the All-Present	טוֹבָה כְפוּלָה וּמְכֻפֶּלֶת, לַמָּקוֹם
for all He did for us!	עָלֵינוּ.
He did bring us out of Egypt.	שֶׁהוֹצִיאָנוּ מִמִּצְרַיִם,

[76] He could have provided us with earthly food, such as herbs or other vegetation (*Rashbam*).

[77] Shabbos is one of the most precious gifts that we received from God and is described as being a sign and an everlasting covenant between God and Israel as it is said, בֵּינִי וּבֵין בְּנֵי יִשְׂרָאֵל אוֹת הִיא לְעוֹלָם (*Metsudos Avraham*).

[78] He could have merely given us the Ten Commandments, or simply added a number of mitzvos to the seven Noachide laws, which had previously been given to the descendants of Noah (*Rashbam*).

He did execute judgments against them.	וְעָשָׂה בָהֶם שְׁפָטִים,
He did execute judgments against their gods.	וְעָשָׂה בֵאלֹהֵיהֶם,
He did slay their firstborn.	וְהָרַג אֶת־בְּכוֹרֵיהֶם,
He did give us their wealth.	וְנָתַן לָנוּ אֶת־מָמוֹנָם,
He did split the Sea for us.	וְקָרַע לָנוּ אֶת־הַיָּם,
He did lead us through it on dry land.	וְהֶעֱבִירָנוּ בְתוֹכוֹ בֶּחָרָבָה,
He did drown our oppressors in it.	וְשִׁקַּע צָרֵינוּ בְּתוֹכוֹ,
He did take care of our needs in the desert for forty years.	וְסִפֵּק צָרְכֵּנוּ בַּמִּדְבָּר אַרְבָּעִים שָׁנָה,
He did feed us the *manna*.	וְהֶאֱכִילָנוּ אֶת־הַמָּן,
He did give us the Shabbos.	וְנָתַן לָנוּ אֶת־הַשַּׁבָּת,
He did bring us to Mount Sinai.	וְקֵרְבָנוּ לִפְנֵי הַר־סִינַי,
He did give us the Torah.	וְנָתַן לָנוּ אֶת־הַתּוֹרָה,
He did bring us into Eretz Yisroel.	וְהִכְנִיסָנוּ לְאֶרֶץ יִשְׂרָאֵל,
He did build the Sanctuary for us,	וּבָנָה לָנוּ אֶת־בֵּית הַבְּחִירָה
to atone for all our sins.	לְכַפֵּר עַל־כָּל־עֲוֹנוֹתֵינוּ.

Rabban Gamliel used to say:	רַבָּן גַּמְלִיאֵל הָיָה אוֹמֵר:
"Anyone who has not said [explained][79]	כָּל־שֶׁלֹּא־אָמַר
these three things at the Pesach [Seder]	שְׁלֹשָׁה דְבָרִים אֵלּוּ בַּפֶּסַח,
has not fulfilled his obligation.	לֹא־יָצָא יְדֵי חוֹבָתוֹ.

---

[79] This emphasis on explanation distinguishes this night from other nights, since our tradition stresses deeds, the actual performance of mitzvos, rather than the discussion of them. Our forefathers declared at Sinai נַעֲשֶׂה וְנִשְׁמַע, *we will do* and we will listen. Nevertheless, in the debate over the relative importance of study and practice, Rabbi Akiva stated that study is more important, since learning about mitzvos leads to performance of mitzvos. At the Seder we do both. We discuss the reasons for the *matzoh* and *morror* and we eat the *matzoh* and *morror*. Thus we learn the lessons of Pesach and we fulfill the mitzvos of Pesach with concrete actions (*Lekutei Avrohom*).

These three things are: :וְאֵלוּ הֵן

the *Pesach* sacrificial offering, *matzoh* .פֶּסַח. מַצָּה

and *morror*. :וּמָרוֹר

The Pesach offering that our fathers ate[80] פֶּסַח שֶׁהָיוּ אֲבוֹתֵינוּ אוֹכְלִים,

when the Beis HaMikdash still stood— בִּזְמַן שֶׁבֵּית־הַמִּקְדָּשׁ קַיָּם,

Why did they do so? עַל־שׁוּם מָה?

[It was eaten] because עַל־שׁוּם,

the Holy One, Blessed is He, passed over שֶׁפָּסַח הַקָּדוֹשׁ בָּרוּךְ הוּא,

the houses of our fathers in Egypt. עַל־בָּתֵּי אֲבוֹתֵינוּ בְּמִצְרַיִם.

as it is said, (*Shemos* 12:27), :שֶׁנֶּאֱמַר

"You shall say וַאֲמַרְתֶּם

'It is the Pesach offering to Adonoy זֶבַח־פֶּסַח הוּא לַיָי,

Who passed over אֲשֶׁר פָּסַח

the houses of the Bnei Yisroel in Egypt עַל־בָּתֵּי בְנֵי־יִשְׂרָאֵל בְּמִצְרַיִם,

when He struck the Egyptians בְּנָגְפּוֹ אֶת־מִצְרַיִם,

and He saved our homes. וְאֶת־בָּתֵּינוּ הִצִּיל.

The people then bowed וַיִּקֹּד הָעָם

and prostrated themselves.' "[81] :וַיִּשְׁתַּחֲווּ

---

[80] At the risk of dreadful reprisals from the Egyptians who held the lamb sacred, the Jews meticulously prepared the *korban pesach* and meticulously observed *that first Pesach in Egypt.* It was a night of vigilance and unease as tragically so many Pesach nights were to be. In times of danger, with bloodthirsty mobs screaming at the door, amid bullets and bombs, Jews strove to observe the Seder. Among survivors of the Holocaust are scraps of paper, makeshift Haggados written by hand, written by heart, written within sight of the smoking crematoria (*Metsudas Avraham*).

[81] They bowed and prostrated themselves in thanksgiving for the tidings of their approaching deliverance, and for the promise of their coming into the land of Israel, and for the tidings regarding the children that they would have. (See verses 25 and 26) (*Rashi*).

*At the words MATZOH ZU (this Matzoh), the Seder leader points to
the Matzos on the Seder plate. Some have the custom to take the Matzoh
in hand and actually show it to the participants.*

This matzoh, that we eat—	מַצָּה זוֹ שֶׁאָנוּ אוֹכְלִים
why do we eat it?	עַל־שׁוּם מָה?
[We eat it] because	עַל־שׁוּם,
even before the dough of our fathers	שֶׁלֹּא הִסְפִּיק בְּצֵקָם שֶׁל אֲבוֹתֵינוּ
had time to become leavened,	לְהַחֲמִיץ,
He revealed himself to them—	עַד שֶׁנִּגְלָה עֲלֵיהֶם,
the supreme King of kings,	מֶלֶךְ מַלְכֵי הַמְּלָכִים
the Holy One, Blessed is He,	הַקָּדוֹשׁ בָּרוּךְ הוּא,
and redeemed them,	וּגְאָלָם.
as it is said, (*Shemos* 12:39),	שֶׁנֶּאֱמַר:
"They baked the dough	וַיֹּאפוּ אֶת־הַבָּצֵק,
that they had brought out of Egypt	אֲשֶׁר הוֹצִיאוּ מִמִּצְרַיִם,
into matzoh cakes, for it was not leavened.	עֻגֹת מַצּוֹת כִּי לֹא חָמֵץ.
Since they were driven out of Egypt	כִּי־גֹרְשׁוּ מִמִּצְרַיִם,
and could not delay,	וְלֹא יָכְלוּ לְהִתְמַהְמֵהַּ,
and also [other] provisions	וְגַם־צֵדָה
they had not prepared for themselves."[82]	לֹא־עָשׂוּ לָהֶם:

---

[82] This is said to tell how praiseworthy the Jews were. They did not say, "How can we go into the wilderness without provisions?" But they had faith and set out to follow God's command. This was the consummate act of faith that the downtrodden slaves manifested, and to which the prophet referred, "זָכַרְתִּי לָךְ חֶסֶד נְעוּרַיִךְ אַהֲבַת כְּלוּלוֹתָיִךְ לֶכְתֵּךְ אַחֲרַי בַּמִּדְבָּר בְּאֶרֶץ לֹא זְרוּעָה, I remember the affection of your youth, the love of your nuptials, how you followed Me into the wilderness, into a land that was not sown" (*Yirmiyahu* 2:2). What was their reward? קֹדֶשׁ יִשְׂרָאֵל לַה' וגו', Israel is Adonoy's hallowed portion" (*Rashi*).

At the words MORROR ZU (this Morror), the Seder leader points to the Morror on the Seder plate. Some have the custom to take the Morror in hand and actually show it to the participants.

This *morror* that we eat—	מָרוֹר זֶה שֶׁאָנוּ אוֹכְלִים
why do we eat it?	עַל־שׁוּם מָה?
[We eat it] because	עַל־שׁוּם,
the Egyptians embittered	שֶׁמָּרְרוּ הַמִּצְרִים
the lives of our fathers in Egypt,[83]	אֶת־חַיֵּי אֲבוֹתֵינוּ בְּמִצְרַיִם,
as it is said, (*Shemos* 1:14),	שֶׁנֶּאֱמַר:
"They made their lives bitter	וַיְמָרְרוּ אֶת־חַיֵּיהֶם
with harsh labor,	בַּעֲבֹדָה קָשָׁה,
involving mortar and bricks,	בְּחֹמֶר וּבִלְבֵנִים,
and all kinds of work in the fields.	וּבְכָל־עֲבֹדָה בַּשָּׂדֶה.
All their work	אֵת כָּל־עֲבֹדָתָם,
which they made them do	אֲשֶׁר־עָבְדוּ
[was intended] to break them."[84]	בָהֶם בְּפָרֶךְ:

In each generation	בְּכָל־דּוֹר וָדוֹר
every person should regard himself	חַיָּב אָדָם לִרְאוֹת אֶת־עַצְמוֹ,
as having personally been redeemed	כְּאִלּוּ הוּא יָצָא
from Egypt,[85]	מִמִּצְרָיִם.

[83] This symbol has never lost its pungency, for it has never been in short supply. This serves to sharpen the point: the bitterness of slavery gives way to the sweetness of redemption and freedom. The morror will be replaced by the many splendored taste of manna (*Metsudas Avrohom*).

[84] בְּפָרֶךְ means with hard labor, which crushes the body and shatters it (see *Maseches Sotah* 11b) (*Rashi*).

[85] In essence, all Israel went out of Egypt, just as all Israel stood at Mount Sinai to receive and accept the Torah. The Haggadah is the script of a living phenomenon, not the record of a dead event, and when the Jews recite it, they are performing an act, not merely of rememberance, but of personal identification in the here and now (*Lekutei Avrohom*).

as it is said, (*Shemos* 13:8),   שֶׁנֶּאֱמַר:

"You must tell your son on that day,   וְהִגַּדְתָּ לְבִנְךָ בַּיּוֹם הַהוּא

saying,   לֵאמֹר.

'It is because of this that Adonoy did for *me*[86]   בַּעֲבוּר זֶה, עָשָׂה יְיָ לִי,

when *I* went out of Egypt.'"   בְּצֵאתִי מִמִּצְרָיִם:

Not only our ancestors   לֹא אֶת־אֲבוֹתֵינוּ בִּלְבָד

did the Holy One, Blessed is He, redeem,   גָּאַל הַקָּדוֹשׁ בָּרוּךְ הוּא,

but He also redeemed us with them,   אֶלָּא אַף אוֹתָנוּ גָּאַל עִמָּהֶם.

as it is said, (*Devarim* 6:23)   שֶׁנֶּאֱמַר:

"He brought us out of there   וְאוֹתָנוּ הוֹצִיא מִשָּׁם.

so that He might bring us [to],   לְמַעַן הָבִיא אֹתָנוּ,

and give us the land   לָתֶת לָנוּ אֶת־הָאָרֶץ,

He had promised to our ancestors."   אֲשֶׁר נִשְׁבַּע לַאֲבֹתֵינוּ:

The matzos are covered, the wine cup is lifted
during the recitation of the following paragraph

Therefore it is our duty   לְפִיכָךְ, אֲנַחְנוּ חַיָּבִים

to thank, to extol, to praise   לְהוֹדוֹת, לְהַלֵּל, לְשַׁבֵּחַ,

to glorify, to exalt, to honor   לְפָאֵר, לְרוֹמֵם, לְהַדֵּר,

to bless, to elevate, and to acclaim   לְבָרֵךְ, לְעַלֵּה וּלְקַלֵּס,

Him, Who performed for our fathers and for us   לְמִי שֶׁעָשָׂה לַאֲבוֹתֵינוּ וְלָנוּ,

all these miracles: אֶת־כָּל־הַנִּסִּים הָאֵלּוּ.

He took us from slavery to freedom,   הוֹצִיאָנוּ מֵעַבְדוּת לְחֵרוּת.

from despair to joy,   מִיָּגוֹן לְשִׂמְחָה.

from mourning to celebration,   וּמֵאֵבֶל לְיוֹם טוֹב.

[86] It is for the purpose of my fulfilling His commands such as this Pesach offering, this matzoh and this *morror,* that God did this for me (*Rashi*).

from darkness to brilliant light,[87]	וּמֵאֲפֵלָה לְאוֹר גָּדוֹל.
from enslavement to redemption.	וּמִשִׁעְבּוּד לִגְאֻלָּה.
Let us [therefore] sing before Him a new song	וְנֹאמַר לְפָנָיו שִׁירָה חֲדָשָׁה,
Halleluyah.	הַלְלוּיָהּ:

The wine cup is set down and the matzos are uncovered

Praise God!

	הַלְלוּיָהּ.
Praise, you servants of Adonoy,[88]	הַלְלוּ עַבְדֵי יְיָ,
praise the Name of Adonoy.	הַלְלוּ אֶת־שֵׁם יְיָ:
The Name of Adonoy will be blessed	יְהִי שֵׁם יְיָ מְבֹרָךְ.
from now forever.	מֵעַתָּה וְעַד־עוֹלָם:
From the rising sun to its setting,	מִמִּזְרַח־שֶׁמֶשׁ עַד־מְבוֹאוֹ.
praised is the Name of Adonoy.	מְהֻלָּל שֵׁם יְיָ:
High above all nations, is Adonoy,	רָם עַל־כָּל־גּוֹיִם יְיָ,
above the heavens, is His Glory.	עַל הַשָּׁמַיִם כְּבוֹדוֹ:
Who is like Adonoy, our God,	מִי כַּייָ אֱלֹהֵינוּ.
Who dwells on high,	הַמַּגְבִּיהִי לָשָׁבֶת:
[yet] looks down so low[89]	הַמַּשְׁפִּילִי לִרְאוֹת
in the heavens and [upon] the earth?	בַּשָּׁמַיִם וּבָאָרֶץ:

[87] The deliverance from the darkness of Egyptian slavery is vitally important as it paved the way to Sinai, the *brilliant light of Torah,* and Israel's acceptance of its special and distinctive mission. The Seder relates how Israel moved progressively from darkness to light, from the ignorance and shame of idolatry to the glory of its enlightened spiritual adventure (*Metsudas Avraham*).

[88] Servitude is usually accompanied by unhappiness and depression, causing the slaves to seek ways of escaping from their master to attain freedom. Servitude of God, however, brings happiness; the Jew seeks ways to serve God and joyfully accepts the "yoke of Divine Sovereignty."—*Sfas Emes*

[89] Enthroned in the highest heavens, He stoops to regard the most lowly on earth. Rabbi Yochanan said, "In every Scriptural passage where you find the greatness of God mentioned, there you also find mention of His humility. (*Megillah* 31a)

He raises up the poor from the dust,	מְקִימִי מֵעָפָר דָּל.
from dunghills He lifts up the needy,[90]	מֵאַשְׁפֹּת יָרִים אֶבְיוֹן:
to seat [them] with nobles,	לְהוֹשִׁיבִי עִם־נְדִיבִים
with the nobles of His people.	עִם נְדִיבֵי עַמּוֹ:
He returns the barren woman to the home[91]	מוֹשִׁיבִי עֲקֶרֶת הַבַּיִת
[as] a joyful mother of children.	אֵם־הַבָּנִים שְׂמֵחָה,
Praise God!	הַלְלוּיָהּ:

When Israel went out of Egypt,	בְּצֵאת יִשְׂרָאֵל מִמִּצְרָיִם.
the House of Jacob	בֵּית יַעֲקֹב
from a people of an alien language,[92]	מֵעַם לֹעֵז:
Judah became His holy nation,[93]	הָיְתָה יְהוּדָה לְקָדְשׁוֹ.
Israel, His dominion.	יִשְׂרָאֵל מַמְשְׁלוֹתָיו:
The sea saw and fled,	הַיָּם רָאָה וַיָּנֹס.
the Jordan turned back.	הַיַּרְדֵּן יִסֹּב לְאָחוֹר:
The mountains skipped like rams,	הֶהָרִים רָקְדוּ כְאֵילִים.
the hills like young sheep.	גְּבָעוֹת כִּבְנֵי־צֹאן:
What bothers you, sea,	מַה־לְּךָ הַיָּם
that you flee;	כִּי תָנוּס.

90 A דַּל (poor man) has absolutely nothing, whereas an אֶבְיוֹן (a needy person), though in dire need, is slightly better off. The *Vilna Gaon* says that this verse is to be understood in a spiritual sense: God raises up even the spiritually poor person who is completely destitute in terms of *Torah* and *mitzvos*; the spiritually needy person is one who may have some knowledge and good deeds but who has sunk into the dunghill of sin. If he earnestly seeks to repent, God will raise him to such a high level of spiritual purity that he will be seated with the "nobles of His people" (the patriarchs and the prophets).

91 *Metsudas Dovid* translates, "He causes the barren woman to return to the home," explaining that a woman without children spends most of her time outside the house. When God grants her children, He thereby causes her to stay at home, rearing her children.

92 לַעַז refers to any non-Hebraic tongue, לֹעֵז denotes a person who speaks an alien tongue. *Targum Yonasan* interprets עַם לֹעֵז, "a barbaric people."

93 "And you will be unto Me a kingdom of priests and a holy nation."—*Shemos* 19:6

Jordan, that you turn backwards?	הַיַּרְדֵּן תִּסֹּב לְאָחוֹר:
Mountains, that you skip like rams	הֶהָרִים תִּרְקְדוּ כְאֵילִים.
hills, like young sheep?	גְּבָעוֹת כִּבְנֵי־צֹאן:
Tremble, earth, before the Master,[94]	מִלִּפְנֵי אָדוֹן חוּלִי אָרֶץ.
from before the God of Jacob,	מִלִּפְנֵי אֱלוֹהַּ יַעֲקֹב:
Who turns the rock[95]	הַהֹפְכִי הַצּוּר
into a pool of water,	אֲגַם־מָיִם.
the flintstone into a fountain of water.	חַלָּמִישׁ לְמַעְיְנוֹ־מָיִם:

The matzos are covered, and the wine cup is lifted
while reciting the following berachah

Blessed are You Adonoy	בָּרוּךְ אַתָּה יְיָ,
our God, King of the Universe	אֱלֹהֵינוּ מֶלֶךְ הָעוֹלָם,
Who redeemed us	אֲשֶׁר גְּאָלָנוּ
and redeemed our fathers from Egypt	וְגָאַל אֶת־אֲבוֹתֵינוּ מִמִּצְרַיִם,
and brought us to this night	וְהִגִּיעָנוּ הַלַּיְלָה הַזֶּה,
whereon we eat matzoh and *morror*.	לֶאֱכָל־בּוֹ מַצָּה וּמָרוֹר.
So, too, Adonoy our God,	כֵּן, יְיָ אֱלֹהֵינוּ
and God of our fathers,	וֵאלֹהֵי אֲבוֹתֵינוּ,
enable us to celebrate holidays	יַגִּיעֵנוּ לְמוֹעֲדִים
and other festivals	וְלִרְגָלִים אֲחֵרִים,
that are forthcoming, in peace;	הַבָּאִים לִקְרָאתֵנוּ לְשָׁלוֹם,
joyful in the rebuilding	שְׂמֵחִים בְּבִנְיַן
of Your city [Jerusalem][96]	עִירֶךָ,

[94] According to the Sages, the words חוּלִי אָרֶץ indicates a creation, i.e., the birth of the world. The verse is thus translated: "Before the Master, the Creator of the earth."

[95] God made water flow from a rock at Refidim.—*Shemos* 17:6 and *Bamidbar* 20:8–11

[96] The *rebuilding* of Jerusalem began on the day of its destruction. The city was rebuilt in time long before it will be rebuilt in space. We have been *rebuilding* it for nearly two thousand years (*Lekutei Avraham*).

and exultant in Your service. וְשָׂשִׂים בַּעֲבוֹדָתֶךָ,

There we shall partake וְנֹאכַל שָׁם

of the sacrifices and of the Pesach offerings מִן הַזְּבָחִים וּמִן הַפְּסָחִים,

On Saturday night some have the custom to say:

from the Pesach offerings and sacrifices מִן הַפְּסָחִים וּמִן הַזְּבָחִים,

whose blood will be sprinkled אֲשֶׁר יַגִּיעַ דָּמָם,

upon the wall of Your altar for Your acceptance. עַל־קִיר מִזְבַּחֲךָ לְרָצוֹן,

We shall sing a new song[97] of thanks to You וְנוֹדֶה לְךָ שִׁיר חָדָשׁ

for our redemption עַל־גְּאֻלָּתֵנוּ,

and for the emancipation of our souls. וְעַל־פְּדוּת נַפְשֵׁנוּ:

Blessed are You, Adonoy בָּרוּךְ אַתָּה יְיָ,

Who redeemed Israel. גָּאַל יִשְׂרָאֵל:

Everyone should now recite the following berachah
and drink all, or at least most of the second cup of wine
while leaning on their left side:

Blessed are You, Adonoy בָּרוּךְ אַתָּה יְיָ,

our God, King of the Universe, אֱלֹהֵינוּ מֶלֶךְ הָעוֹלָם,

Creator of the fruit of the vine. בּוֹרֵא, פְּרִי הַגָּפֶן:

---

[97] We are engaged in what is probably the oldest ritual of its kind, the Seder, a ritual with a virtually unbroken tradition of observance for well over three thousand years. Yet there is nothing routine about this Seder ritual, nothing remiss about our performance of its mitzvos. This is why the Haggadah exclaims, "We shall sing a *new song*, for every year it is a new, fresh experience in our lives. Our rejoicing about the redemption increases the power of the Almighty and His hosts in the heavenly regions above, just as an earthly king gains in power and stature when his subjects broadcast his fame far and wide (*Lekutei Avraham*).

Rochtzah רָחְצָה

Take a cup or pitcher of water in one hand and pour it over the other hand, three times. Then reverse hands and do the same to your other hand. The following berachah is said before drying the hands:

Blessed are You, Adonoy	בָּרוּךְ אַתָּה יְיָ,
our God, King of the universe	אֱלֹהֵינוּ מֶלֶךְ הָעוֹלָם,
Who sanctified us with His commandments	אֲשֶׁר קִדְּשָׁנוּ בְּמִצְוֹתָיו,
and commanded us	וְצִוָּנוּ
concerning washing the hands.	עַל־נְטִילַת יָדָיִם:

It is not permitted to talk between washing and eating the matzoh, and this applies also to the matzoh that will be eaten together with the morror in a sandwich.

Motzi מוֹצִיא

The Seder leader takes the matzos from the seder plate, holding the broken matzoh between the two whole matzos and says this berachah:

Blessed are you, Adonoy	בָּרוּךְ אַתָּה יְיָ,
our God, King of the universe	אֱלֹהֵינוּ מֶלֶךְ הָעוֹלָם,
Who brings forth bread from the earth.	הַמּוֹצִיא לֶחֶם מִן־הָאָרֶץ:

Matzoh מַצָּה

The Seder leader lowers the bottom matzoh and holding the top and the broken (middle matzoh) says this berachah (keeping in mind that matzoh will also be eaten in the sandwich)

Blessed are you	בָּרוּךְ אַתָּה יְיָ,
Adonoy, King of the universe	אֱלֹהֵינוּ מֶלֶךְ הָעוֹלָם,
Who sanctified us with His commandments	אֲשֶׁר קִדְּשָׁנוּ בְּמִצְוֹתָיו,
and commanded us concerning eating matzoh.	וְצִוָּנוּ עַל־אֲכִילַת מַצָּה:

He then takes a piece of the top and of the broken matzoh, (preferably a *k'zayis* of each, but at least one *k'zayis* combined). A *k'zayis* of hand-made matzoh is about 4 inches by 7 inches. (A *k'zayis* of machine matzoh is about two thirds of a matzoh.) He gives similar portions of matzoh to all the participants. He then eats both pieces of matzoh while leaning on his left side, and so do the participants, after reciting the two previous *berachos*. **Each *k'zayis* should be eaten within a maximum time frame of four minutes.**

Morror מָרוֹר

The Seder leader takes a *K'zayis* of *morror* (an amount of ground horse-raddish that can be compacted into a volume of 1.1 fluid ounces; or an amount of romaine lettuce that covers an area of 8 by 10 inches), dips it into the *charoses*, then shakes all the *charoses* off the *morror*; and gives similar portions to every Seder participant. (The *charoses*, which is a mixture of apples, nuts, etc., is used only to soften the sharpness of the *morror*, but it must *not* be eaten with the *morror*.

Everyone then recites the following berachah (keeping in mind that the *morror* will also be eaten with the sandwich):

Blessed are you, Adonoy	בָּרוּךְ אַתָּה יְיָ,
our God, King of the Universe	אֱלֹהֵינוּ מֶלֶךְ הָעוֹלָם,
Who sanctified us with His commandments	אֲשֶׁר קִדְּשָׁנוּ בְּמִצְוֹתָיו,
and commanded us concerning eating *morror*.	וְצִוָּנוּ עַל־אֲכִילַת מָרוֹר:

The *morror* should be eaten *without reclining* since it commemorates the bitterness of slavery and does not signify freedom. As when eating the matzoh, the *morror* should be eaten without delay or interruption, and must be *chewed* before swallowing.

Koreich כּוֹרֵךְ

The Seder leader takes the bottom, unbroken matzoh, breaks off a *k'zayis* size piece and together with a *k'zayis* of *morror,* makes a sandwich. (Some have the custom of also dipping this *morror* in *charoses,* but others do not do so). Similar portions are given to every Seder participant and everyone eats this sandwich while reclining on their left side after reciting the following:

As a reminder of the *Mikdosh* (Temple),	זֵכֶר לְמִקְדָּשׁ
we follow the practice of Hillel;	כְּהִלֵּל.
this is what Hillel would do[98]	כֵּן עָשָׂה הִלֵּל,
while the *Beis Mikdosh* still existed.	בִּזְמַן שֶׁבֵּית הַמִּקְדָּשׁ הָיָה קַיָּם.
He would make a sandwich	הָיָה כּוֹרֵךְ
of matzoh and morror	מַצָּה וּמָרוֹר

Some Haggadahs include the word פסח, because Hillel would add a piece of the roasted Pesach offering in the sandwich.

And eat them together	וְאוֹכֵל בְּיָחַד.
to fulfill what is said, (Bamidbar 9:11),	לְקַיֵּם מַה שֶׁנֶּאֱמַר:
"With matzoh and *morror* you shall eat it."	עַל־מַצּוֹת וּמְרֹרִים יֹאכְלֻהוּ:

This sandwich also must be eaten promptly, without interruptions, as when eating the previous k'zayis *of matzoh and of* morror.

[98] There is a disagreement over whether matzoh and *morror* and the Pesach offering were eaten together in a sandwich during Temple times, or whether each was eaten separately. Hillel took the position that they must be eaten in a sandwich rather than separately. In our days, the Pesach offering is not eaten, but in remembrance of Hillel's opinion, we eat a matzoh-*morror* sandwich after we have fulfilled the *mitzvah* of matzoh and of *morror* by eating each separately.

Shulchan Oreich   שֻׁלְחָן עוֹרֵךְ

The Yom Tov meal is now served. Tonight's meal with its unique setting and its unusual ingredients, is itself an occasion for festive rejoicing. In fact, since Hallel psalms are said before and after the meal, the *Netziv* and others, consider this meal to be part of Hallel, a distinct act of praise. Therefore we should sing זְמִירוֹת, songs of praise, discuss the laws and legends of Pesach, and refrain from idle conversation.

The Hard Boiled Egg   בֵּיצָה

It is customary to begin the meal with a hard-boiled egg. A number of reasons are given for this custom. The egg is the symbol of mourning, it being completely smooth, without an opening and thus compared to the mourner who bears his grief in silence. This is also symbolic of our painful awareness of the lack of the Pesach sacrifice and reminds us of the destruction of the *Beis HaMikdosh*, particularly since the fast commemorating its destruction, *Tisha B'Av*, always occurs on the same day of the week as the first night of Pesach.

Broiled or roasted meat must not be eaten at the Seder, since the Pesach offering which we do not have, had to be roasted.

The meal should be completed in time for the *afikoman* to be eaten before midnight. Care should be taken not to eat so heavily that you will be unable to eat the *afikoman* with appetite, or that you will be drowsy for the conclusion of the Seder.

Tzafun[99] צָפוּן

It is now that we eat the *afikoman*. The *afikoman* is a symbol of the Pesach offering which was eaten at the conclusion of the meal when people are no longer hungry. The meaning of the word *afikoman* is unclear, but it probably means dessert, and since the Seder meal must conclude with matzoh, the matzoh itself came to be called *afikoman*. *In order for the taste of the matzoh to linger in our mouths,*[100] *we are not permitted to eat or drink after eating the afikoman, except of course, the last two cups of wine.* (After the Seder is concluded, it is permitted to drink water, tea, or other light beverage if you are thirsty.)

The Seder leader takes the piece of matzoh that he had hidden at the beginning of the Seder.[101] He then takes from it a *k'zayis* and gives each participant a *k'zayis* (by adding other pieces of *matzoh* to the *afikoman* matzoh to equal a *k'zayis*) and all eat it while leaning on their left side. *It should be eaten promptly without interruption,* as previously stated in reference to the eating of the matzoh and *morror*. According to most *halachic* opinions, the *afikoman* should be eaten before midnight.

---

[99] Tzafun actually refers to something that is concealed. The hiddenness of the *afikoman* intimates to us that the miracle of the Exodus was merely a preparation for the future redemption which is still concealed from us (*Lekutei Avrohom*).

[100] Our ultimate redemption depends on keeping the taste of matzoh,—the experience of slavery and redemption from Egypt—in our mouths. We must diligently strive to remember and strengthen the spiritial freedom the Almighty granted us when He took us to be His slaves. There is no greater freedom than service to Gd, and no freer man than a slave to the Almighty.

[101] It is the larger piece of the middle matzoh that is concealed, for much more is hidden than revealed. We prepared for Pesach by searching, for hidden *chametz*; we conclude the Seder by searching for the hidden matzoh. To know there is *concealment* is to know there is also *revelation* for which we must strive and pray. May we be worthy of the great and ultimate revelation of כְּבוֹד שָׁמַיִם, the glory of God. (*Lekutei Avrohom*)

Bareich   בָּרֵךְ

Birkas Hamazon   בִּרְכַּת הַמָּזוֹן

The third cup of wine is filled

A Song of Ascents.	שִׁיר הַמַּעֲלוֹת
When Adonoy brings about the return to Zion	בְּשׁוּב יְיָ אֶת־שִׁיבַת צִיּוֹן
we will have been like dreamers.[1]	הָיִינוּ כְּחֹלְמִים:
Then will our mouths be filled with laughter,[2]	אָז יִמָּלֵא שְׂחוֹק פִּינוּ
and our tongue with joyous song.	וּלְשׁוֹנֵנוּ רִנָּה
Then will they say among the nations:	אָז יֹאמְרוּ בַגּוֹיִם
'Adonoy had done great things for them.'	הִגְדִּיל יְיָ לַעֲשׂוֹת עִם־אֵלֶּה:
Adonoy has done great things for us;	הִגְדִּיל יְיָ לַעֲשׂוֹת עִמָּנוּ
we will [then] rejoice.	הָיִינוּ שְׂמֵחִים:
Adonoy! bring back our exiles	שׁוּבָה יְיָ אֶת־שְׁבִיתֵנוּ
like springs in the desert.[3]	כַּאֲפִיקִים בַּנֶּגֶב:
Those who sow in tears	הַזֹּרְעִים בְּדִמְעָה
will reap with joyous song.[4]	בְּרִנָּה יִקְצֹרוּ:

[1] Upon the redemption and return to Zion, the harshness of the exile will seem to the Jews like a terrible dream.—*Radak.*

The splendor of the return to Zion will be like the realization of an impossible dream.—*Seporno.*

[2] In the Talmud (*Maseches Berachos* 31a) Rabbi Shimon bar Yochai rules that a Jew is forbidden to fill his mouth with laughter in this world until the time comes when all nations declare: "Adonoy has done great things for them"—as the verse states: אָז *then*: only then, when God's love for us is universally recognized, may we experience total exultation.

[3] Just as springs of water can transform an arid desert into a fertile oasis, so will we be transformed, and flourish when God delivers us from exile.—*Rashi*

[4] A person who plants in desert-like soil is always fearful that his crops will not grow. If a spring of water should suddenly appear on his land, his joy will know no bounds. So great will our joy be at the ultimate redemption that will follow the oppression of exile.—*Radak*

[Though] he walks along weeping,	הָלוֹךְ יֵלֵךְ וּבָכֹה
carrying the bag of seed,	נֹשֵׂא מֶשֶׁךְ־הַזָּרַע
he will return with joyous song	בֹּא־יָבֹא בְרִנָּה
carrying his sheaves.	נֹשֵׂא אֲלֻמֹּתָיו:

When three or more males, aged 13 or older eat together one of them leads the group in reciting the Birkas Hamazon.

The leader begins by saying:

"Gentlemen, let us say the blessing:	רַבּוֹתַי נְבָרֵךְ:

The others respond:

"The Name of Adonoy will be blessed	יְהִי שֵׁם יְיָ מְבֹרָךְ
from now forever."	מֵעַתָּה וְעַד עוֹלָם:

The leader repeats:

"The Name of Adonoy will be blessed	יְהִי שֵׁם יְיָ מְבֹרָךְ
from now forever."	מֵעַתָּה וְעַד עוֹלָם:

The leader continues: (the words "our God" are substituted for "Him" and "He" if ten males are in the group):

"With your permission	בִּרְשׁוּת
our masters and teachers,	מָרָנָן וְרַבּוֹתַי,
Let us bless (our God,) Him,	נְבָרֵךְ (אֱלֹהֵינוּ)
for we have eaten of His bounty."	שֶׁאָכַלְנוּ מִשֶּׁלוֹ:

The others respond accordingly:

"Blessed is (our God) He	בָּרוּךְ (אֱלֹהֵינוּ)
for we have eaten of His bounty	שֶׁאָכַלְנוּ מִשֶּׁלּוֹ
and through His goodness we live."	וּבְטוּבוֹ חָיִינוּ:

The leader repeats:

"Blessed is (our God) He	בָּרוּךְ (אֱלֹהֵינוּ)
for we have eaten of His bounty	שֶׁאָכַלְנוּ מִשֶּׁלּוֹ
and through His goodness we live."	וּבְטוּבוֹ חָיִינוּ:

If there are at least 10 men, add:

"Blessed is He and blessed is His Name."	בָּרוּךְ הוּא וּבָרוּךְ שְׁמוֹ:

Blessed are You, Adonoy	בָּרוּךְ אַתָּה יְיָ,
our God, King of the Universe,	אֱלֹהֵינוּ מֶלֶךְ הָעוֹלָם,
Who nourishes the entire world	הַזָּן אֶת־הָעוֹלָם כֻּלּוֹ,
with His goodness,	בְּטוּבוֹ,
with favor, with kindness, and with mercy.[5]	בְּחֵן בְּחֶסֶד וּבְרַחֲמִים,
He provides food for all flesh,[6]	הוּא נוֹתֵן לֶחֶם לְכָל־בָּשָׂר
for His kindness endures forever.	כִּי לְעוֹלָם חַסְדּוֹ.
And through His great goodness,	וּבְטוּבוֹ הַגָּדוֹל,
we have never lacked	תָּמִיד לֹא־חָסַר לָנוּ,

---

[5] The righteous find *favor* in the eyes of God and are nourished because of their merit. Those who are not so worthy and do not find favor, are provided for through God's beneficent *kindness;* while even the least worthy are recipients of God's *mercy.*—Maharal in *Nesivos Olom*

[6] This citation from *Psalms* 136:25 indicates that God's kindness and compassion are universal, relating to all flesh, including animals.—*Avudraham.*

and we will not lack food	וְאַל־יֶחְסַר לָנוּ מָזוֹן
forever and ever,	לְעוֹלָם וָעֶד.
for the sake of His great Name.	בַּעֲבוּר שְׁמוֹ הַגָּדוֹל,
For He is Almighty	כִּי הוּא אֵל
Who nourishes[7] and maintains all,	זָן וּמְפַרְנֵס לַכֹּל
does good to all, and prepares nourishment	וּמֵטִיב לַכֹּל וּמֵכִין מָזוֹן
for all His creatures which He has created.	לְכָל־בְּרִיּוֹתָיו אֲשֶׁר בָּרָא:
Blessed are You, Adonoy	בָּרוּךְ אַתָּה יְיָ,
Who nourishes all.[8]	הַזָּן אֶת־הַכֹּל:
We thank You, Adonoy, our God,	נוֹדֶה לְךָ יְיָ אֱלֹהֵינוּ
for Your parceling out as a heritage	עַל שֶׁהִנְחַלְתָּ
to our fathers,	לַאֲבוֹתֵינוּ,
a land[9] which is desirable, good, and spacious;	אֶרֶץ חֶמְדָּה טוֹבָה וּרְחָבָה,
for Your bringing us out, Adonoy, our God,	וְעַל שֶׁהוֹצֵאתָנוּ, יְיָ אֱלֹהֵינוּ,
from the land of Egypt,	מֵאֶרֶץ מִצְרַיִם,
and redeeming us from the house of bondage;	וּפְדִיתָנוּ מִבֵּית עֲבָדִים.

[7] "Nourishes" refers to food, "maintains" refers to clothing and "does good" refers to shelter. These are the basic needs of man, all of which God provides.—*Etz Yosef*

[8] The first blessing of the *Birkas Hamazon* was composed by Moses in appreciation for the *manna* which God provided for the Jews in the desert.

The second blessing, beginning with "Let us thank You," was composed by Joshua in gratitude for the privilege of entering the Promised Land.

The third blessing, beginning with "Have mercy," was composed by David who conquered Jerusalem, and by Solomon who built the Temple.

The fourth blessing "Who is good and beneficent to all" was composed by Rabban Gamliel the Elder and his court in Yavneh in gratitude to God for preserving the bodies of the victims of the Roman massacre at Betar, and for being enabled to bring them to proper burial.—*Maseches Berachos 48b*

[9] The land is mentioned even before the Exodus from Egypt because God demonstrated His extraordinary concern for the Jewish people at the very beginning of their history; first by the promise He gave to the Patriarchs concerning the Land of Israel and then, with the fulfillment of that promise, once He redeemed them from Egypt to enter the Land.—*S.R. Hirsch*

for Your covenant וְעַל בְּרִיתְךָ

which You sealed in our flesh; שֶׁחָתַמְתָּ בִּבְשָׂרֵנוּ,

for Your Torah[10] which You taught us; וְעַל תּוֹרָתְךָ שֶׁלִּמַּדְתָּנוּ,

for Your statutes וְעַל חֻקֶּיךָ

which You made known to us; שֶׁהוֹדַעְתָּנוּ,

for the life, favor, and kindness וְעַל חַיִּים חֵן וָחֶסֶד

which You granted us; שֶׁחוֹנַנְתָּנוּ,

and for the provision of food וְעַל אֲכִילַת מָזוֹן

with which You nourish and maintain us שָׁאַתָּה זָן וּמְפַרְנֵס אוֹתָנוּ

constantly, every day, at all times תָּמִיד, בְּכָל־יוֹם וּבְכָל־עֵת

and in every hour. וּבְכָל־שָׁעָה:

For everything Adonoy, our God. וְעַל הַכֹּל יְיָ אֱלֹהֵינוּ,

We thank You אֲנַחְנוּ מוֹדִים לָךְ,

and bless You. וּמְבָרְכִים אוֹתָךְ,

Blessed be Your Name יִתְבָּרַךְ שִׁמְךָ,

through the mouth of all the living. בְּפִי כָל־חַי,

constantly, forever, as it is written: תָּמִיד לְעוֹלָם וָעֶד. כַּכָּתוּב,

"When You have eaten and are satisfied, וְאָכַלְתָּ וְשָׂבָעְתָּ,

You will bless Adonoy, your God, וּבֵרַכְתָּ אֶת־יְיָ אֱלֹהֶיךָ,

for the good land עַל־הָאָרֶץ הַטֹּבָה

which He has given to you."[11] אֲשֶׁר־נָתַן לָךְ:

Blessed are You, Adonoy, בָּרוּךְ אַתָּה יְיָ,

for the land and for the food. עַל הָאָרֶץ וְעַל הַמָּזוֹן:

---

[10] "Torah" refers to laws which are comprehensible to the human intellect; it is therefore *taught*. "Statutes" חֻקִּים are beyond human understanding and are therefore merely *made known* to man, for man cannot comprehend them. *Eyun Tefilloh*

[11] Deuteronomy 8:10

Have compassion, Adonoy, our God,	רַחֶם־נָא יְיָ אֱלֹהֵינוּ,
on Israel, Your people,	עַל יִשְׂרָאֵל עַמֶּךָ,
on Jerusalem, Your city,	וְעַל יְרוּשָׁלַיִם עִירֶךָ,
on Zion, the dwelling place of Your glory,	וְעַל צִיּוֹן מִשְׁכַּן כְּבוֹדֶךָ,
on the kingship of the house of David,	וְעַל מַלְכוּת בֵּית דָּוִד
Your anointed;	מְשִׁיחֶךָ,
and on the great and holy House	וְעַל הַבַּיִת הַגָּדוֹל וְהַקָּדוֹשׁ
upon which Your Name is called.	שֶׁנִּקְרָא שִׁמְךָ עָלָיו.
Our God, our Father, tend us, nourish us,[12]	אֱלֹהֵינוּ, אָבִינוּ, רְעֵנוּ, זוּנֵנוּ,
maintain us, sustain us, relieve us[13]	פַּרְנְסֵנוּ, וְכַלְכְּלֵנוּ, וְהַרְוִיחֵנוּ,
and grant us relief Adonoy, our God,	וְהַרְוַח־לָנוּ יְיָ אֱלֹהֵינוּ
speedily from all our troubles.	מְהֵרָה מִכָּל־צָרוֹתֵינוּ.
Adonoy, our God—may we never be in need	וְנָא, אַל־תַּצְרִיכֵנוּ יְיָ אֱלֹהֵינוּ
of the gifts of men	לֹא לִידֵי מַתְּנַת בָּשָׂר וָדָם,
nor of their loans,	וְלֹא לִידֵי הַלְוָאָתָם,
but only of Your hand which is full, open,	כִּי אִם לְיָדְךָ הַמְּלֵאָה, הַפְּתוּחָה,
holy and generous,	הַקְּדוֹשָׁה וְהָרְחָבָה,
so that we may not be shamed or humiliated[14]	שֶׁלֹּא נֵבוֹשׁ וְלֹא נִכָּלֵם
forever and ever.	לְעוֹלָם וָעֶד:

If you forgot to say יַעֲלֶה וְיָבֹא or רְצֵה and became aware of it before starting the fourth berachah הַטּוֹב וְהַמֵּטִיב, see pages 64 and 65 for the appropriate berachos.

---

[12] "Tend us" by providing the basic necessities of life such as bread and water; "nourish" us with an enriched diet including foods such as fruits and vegetables.—*Etz Yosef*

[13] "Maintain us" with food and shelter; "sustain us" by providing our needs on a regular basis, not on a feast or famine cycle; and "relieve us" by giving us ample means to live comfortably.—*Etz Yosef*

[14] May we not be "ashamed" in this world due to poverty and may we not be "humiliated" in the World-to-Come, because of our transgressions. Poverty often brings shame which in turn might cause a person to lose faith.—*Etz Yosef*

On Shabbos add:

May it please You, to strengthen us	רְצֵה וְהַחֲלִיצֵנוּ
Adonoy, our God,	יְיָ אֱלֹהֵינוּ,
through Your commandments,	בְּמִצְוֹתֶיךָ,
and through the commandment	וּבְמִצְוַת
of the seventh day,	יוֹם הַשְּׁבִיעִי
this great and holy Sabbath.	הַשַּׁבָּת הַגָּדוֹל וְהַקָּדוֹשׁ הַזֶּה.
For this day	כִּי יוֹם זֶה,
is great and holy before You,	גָּדוֹל וְקָדוֹשׁ הוּא לְפָנֶיךָ,
to refrain from work on it	לִשְׁבָּת־בּוֹ
and to rest on it with love,	וְלָנוּחַ בּוֹ, בְּאַהֲבָה,
as ordained by Your will.	כְּמִצְוַת רְצוֹנֶךָ.
And by Your will,	וּבִרְצוֹנְךָ
grant us repose Adonoy, our God,	הָנִיחַ לָנוּ יְיָ אֱלֹהֵינוּ,
that there be no distress, sorrow,	שֶׁלֹּא תְהֵא צָרָה וְיָגוֹן
or sighing on the day of our rest.[15]	וַאֲנָחָה, בְּיוֹם מְנוּחָתֵנוּ.
Show us Adonoy, our God,	וְהַרְאֵנוּ, יְיָ אֱלֹהֵינוּ,
the consolation of Zion, Your city,	בְּנֶחָמַת צִיּוֹן עִירֶךָ,
and the rebuilding of Jerusalem,	וּבְבִנְיַן יְרוּשָׁלַיִם
city of Your Sanctuary,	עִיר קָדְשֶׁךָ,
for You are the Master of deliverance	כִּי אַתָּה הוּא, בַּעַל הַיְשׁוּעוֹת,
and the Master of consolation.	וּבַעַל הַנֶּחָמוֹת:

[15] Even though prayers for personal needs are not recited on Shabbos, this particular prayer does contain such a request, because it is so closely interwoven with the commandment to rest on Shabbos. Since we are commanded to make Shabbos a day of sacred rest, we ask that our repose not be desecrated by distress or misfortune.—*Avudraham*

Our God and God of our fathers,	אֱלֹהֵינוּ וֵאלֹהֵי אֲבוֹתֵינוּ,
may there ascend, come, and reach,	יַעֲלֶה וְיָבֹא, וְיַגִּיעַ,
appear, be desired, and heard,	וְיֵרָאֶה, וְיֵרָצֶה, וְיִשָּׁמַע,
counted and recalled	וְיִפָּקֵד, וְיִזָּכֵר,
our remembrance and reckoning;	זִכְרוֹנֵנוּ וּפִקְדוֹנֵנוּ,
the remembrance of our fathers;	וְזִכְרוֹן אֲבוֹתֵינוּ,
the remembrance of the Moshiach	וְזִכְרוֹן מָשִׁיחַ
the son of David, Your servant;	בֶּן־דָּוִד עַבְדֶּךָ,
the remembrance of Jerusalem,	וְזִכְרוֹן יְרוּשָׁלַיִם
city of Your Sanctuary,	עִיר קָדְשֶׁךָ,
and the remembrance of Your entire people,	וְזִכְרוֹן כָּל־עַמְּךָ
the House of Israel, before You,	בֵּית יִשְׂרָאֵל, לְפָנֶיךָ.
for survival, for well-being,	לִפְלֵיטָה, לְטוֹבָה,
for favor, kindliness, compassion,	לְחֵן וּלְחֶסֶד וּלְרַחֲמִים,
for life and peace	לְחַיִּים וּלְשָׁלוֹם,
on this day of	בְּיוֹם
the Festival of Matzos	חַג הַמַּצּוֹת הַזֶּה.
Remember us Adonoy, our God	זָכְרֵנוּ יְיָ אֱלֹהֵינוּ,
on this day for well-being;	בּוֹ לְטוֹבָה,
be mindful of us on this day for blessing,	וּפָקְדֵנוּ בוֹ לִבְרָכָה,
and deliver us for life.	וְהוֹשִׁיעֵנוּ בוֹ לְחַיִּים.
In accord with the promise of deliverance	וּבִדְבַר יְשׁוּעָה
and compassion,	וְרַחֲמִים,
spare us and favor us,	חוּס וְחָנֵּנוּ,
have compassion on us and deliver us;	וְרַחֵם עָלֵינוּ וְהוֹשִׁיעֵנוּ,
for to You our eyes are directed	כִּי אֵלֶיךָ עֵינֵינוּ,
because You are the Almighty	כִּי אֵל
Who is King, Gracious, and Merciful.	מֶלֶךְ חַנּוּן וְרַחוּם אָתָּה:

Rebuild Jerusalem, city of the Holy Sanctuary,	וּבְנֵה יְרוּשָׁלַיִם עִיר הַקֹּדֶשׁ,
speedily, in our days.	בִּמְהֵרָה בְיָמֵינוּ.
Blessed are You, Adonoy,	בָּרוּךְ אַתָּה יְיָ,
Builder of Jerusalem in His mercy. Amein.[16]	בּוֹנֵה בְרַחֲמָיו יְרוּשָׁלָיִם. אָמֵן:

Blessed are You, Adonoy	בָּרוּךְ אַתָּה יְיָ,
our God, King of the Universe,	אֱלֹהֵינוּ מֶלֶךְ הָעוֹלָם,
the Almighty, our Father, our King,	הָאֵל אָבִינוּ, מַלְכֵּנוּ,
our Mighty One, our Creator, our Redeemer,	אַדִּירֵנוּ, בּוֹרְאֵנוּ, גּוֹאֲלֵנוּ,
our Maker, our Holy One, Holy One of Jacob,	יוֹצְרֵנוּ, קְדוֹשֵׁנוּ, קְדוֹשׁ יַעֲקֹב.
our Shepherd, Shepherd of Israel,	רוֹעֵנוּ רֹעֵה יִשְׂרָאֵל.
the King, Who is good and beneficent to all.	הַמֶּלֶךְ הַטּוֹב, וְהַמֵּטִיב לַכֹּל.
Every single day He has done good,	שֶׁבְּכָל־יוֹם וָיוֹם הוּא הֵטִיב,
does good, and will do good to us.	הוּא מֵטִיב, הוּא יֵיטִיב לָנוּ.
He has rewarded us, He rewards us,	הוּא גְמָלָנוּ. הוּא גוֹמְלֵנוּ.
He will reward us forever with	הוּא יִגְמְלֵנוּ לָעַד
favor, kindness, and compassion,	לְחֵן וּלְחֶסֶד, וּלְרַחֲמִים
relief, rescue, and success,	וּלְרֶוַח, הַצָּלָה וְהַצְלָחָה,
blessing, deliverance, and consolation,	בְּרָכָה וִישׁוּעָה, נֶחָמָה,
maintenance, sustenance, compassion,	פַּרְנָסָה וְכַלְכָּלָה, וְרַחֲמִים,
life, peace, and everything good;	וְחַיִּים וְשָׁלוֹם, וְכָל־טוֹב,
and of all good things	וּמִכָּל־טוּב
may He never deprive us.[17]	לְעוֹלָם אַל־יְחַסְּרֵנוּ:

---

[16] It is unusual for one to answer Amein after his own blessing. This blessing ends with Amein because it marks the end of the three blessings, authority for which is derived from *Deuteronomy* (8:10) and separates them from the next blessing which is Rabbinic in origin.—*Maseches Berachos* 45b

[17] Many people are granted the bounties of life but are unable to enjoy them. We first invoke God's blessing for all the good things in life and then ask Him to grant us the privilege of enjoying them.—*Iyun Tefilloh*.

The Merciful One will reign over us	הָרַחֲמָן, הוּא יִמְלֹךְ עָלֵינוּ
forever and ever.	לְעוֹלָם וָעֶד:
The Merciful One will be blessed	הָרַחֲמָן, הוּא יִתְבָּרַךְ
in heaven and on earth.	בַּשָּׁמַיִם וּבָאָרֶץ:
The Merciful One will be praised	הָרַחֲמָן, הוּא יִשְׁתַּבַּח
for all generations,	לְדוֹר דּוֹרִים,
He will be glorified through us	וְיִתְפָּאַר בָּנוּ לָעַד
forever and for all eternity;	וּלְנֵצַח נְצָחִים,
and He will be honored through us	וְיִתְהַדַּר בָּנוּ לָעַד
for time everlasting.	וּלְעוֹלְמֵי עוֹלָמִים:
May the Merciful One maintain us with honor.	הָרַחֲמָן, הוּא יְפַרְנְסֵנוּ בְּכָבוֹד:
The Merciful One will break the yoke	הָרַחֲמָן, הוּא יִשְׁבֹּר עֻלֵּנוּ
(of oppression) from our necks	מֵעַל צַוָּארֵנוּ,
and lead us upright	וְהוּא יוֹלִיכֵנוּ קוֹמְמִיּוּת
to our land.	לְאַרְצֵנוּ:
May the Merciful One send us	הָרַחֲמָן, הוּא יִשְׁלַח לָנוּ,
abundant blessing to this house,	בְּרָכָה מְרֻבָּה בַּבַּיִת הַזֶּה,
and upon this table	וְעַל שֻׁלְחָן זֶה
at which we have eaten.	שֶׁאָכַלְנוּ עָלָיו:
The Merciful One will send us	הָרַחֲמָן, הוּא יִשְׁלַח לָנוּ,
Elijah the prophet,	אֶת־אֵלִיָּהוּ הַנָּבִיא
who is remembered for good,	זָכוּר לַטּוֹב
who will announce to us	וִיבַשֶּׂר־לָנוּ
good tidings, deliverances,	בְּשׂוֹרוֹת טוֹבוֹת יְשׁוּעוֹת
and consolations.	וְנֶחָמוֹת:

When eating at your parents' table, say:

May the Merciful One bless	הָרַחֲמָן, הוּא יְבָרֵךְ
my father, my teacher,	אֶת־אָבִי מוֹרִי
the master of this house,	בַּעַל הַבַּיִת הַזֶּה,
and my mother, my teacher,	וְאֶת־אִמִּי מוֹרָתִי,
the mistress of this house;	בַּעֲלַת הַבַּיִת הַזֶּה.
them, their household,	אוֹתָם וְאֶת־בֵּיתָם,
their children	וְאֶת־זַרְעָם
and all that is theirs.	וְאֶת־כָּל־אֲשֶׁר לָהֶם.

When eating at your own table, say:

May the Merciful One bless	הָרַחֲמָן, הוּא יְבָרֵךְ
me, my spouse, my children,	אוֹתִי וְאֶת־אִשְׁתִּי וְאֶת זַרְעִי
and all that is mine;	וְאֶת־כָּל־אֲשֶׁר לִי.

A guest says:

May the Merciful One bless	הָרַחֲמָן, הוּא יְבָרֵךְ
the host	בַּעַל הַבַּיִת הַזֶּה,
and the hostess,	וְאֶת־בַּעֲלַת הַבַּיִת הַזֶּה.
them, their household, their children	אוֹתָם וְאֶת־בֵּיתָם וְאֶת־זַרְעָם
and all that is theirs.	וְאֶת־כָּל־אֲשֶׁר לָהֶם.

May[18] it be God's will that the	יְהִי רָצוֹן
host not be shamed	שֶׁלֹא יֵבוֹשׁ בַּעַל הַבַּיִת

---

[18] This blessing is quoted from the talmud (*Maseches Berachos* 46a). It has been omitted in most Siddurim. The Mishnah Berura (201:5) takes issue with its omission. We have incorporated it in this edition.

in this world	בָּעוֹלָם הַזֶּה
or humiliated in the World-to- Come.	וְלֹא יִכָּלֵם לָעוֹלָם הַבָּא
May he have great success	וְיִצְלַח מְאֹד
with all his possessions.	בְּכָל נְכָסָיו
May his properties and ours prosper	וְיִהְיוּ נְכָסָיו וּנְכָסֵינוּ מֻצְלָחִים
and be located close to town.	וּקְרוֹבִים לָעִיר
May no evil force have power over	וְאַל יִשְׁלֹט שָׂטָן
his endeavors	לֹא בְּמַעֲשֵׂי יָדָיו
or our endeavors.	וְלֹא בְּמַעֲשֵׂי יָדֵינוּ
May no opportunity present itself before him	וְאַל יִזְדַּקֵּר לֹא לְפָנָיו
or before us	וְלֹא לְפָנֵינוּ
to contemplate	שׁוּם דְּבַר הִרְהוּר
[committing any] sin, transgression or iniquity	חֵטְא וַעֲבֵרָה וְעָוֹן
from now forever.	מֵעַתָּה וְעַד עוֹלָם:
Ours and all that is ours—	אוֹתָנוּ וְאֶת־כָּל־אֲשֶׁר לָנוּ,
just as our forefathers were blessed—	כְּמוֹ שֶׁנִּתְבָּרְכוּ אֲבוֹתֵינוּ,
Abraham, Isaac, and Jacob—	אַבְרָהָם, יִצְחָק וְיַעֲקֹב,
"In all things,"[19] "From everything,"[20]	בַּכֹּל, מִכֹּל,
and "With everything";[21]	כֹּל.
so may He bless us,	כֵּן יְבָרֵךְ אוֹתָנוּ,
all of us together, with a perfect blessing	כֻּלָּנוּ יַחַד, בִּבְרָכָה שְׁלֵמָה.
and let us say Amein.	וְנֹאמַר אָמֵן:
From on high,	בַּמָּרוֹם
may there be invoked upon them and upon us,	יְלַמְּדוּ עֲלֵיהֶם וְעָלֵינוּ

[19] Abraham was blessed "in all things." *Genesis* 24:1
[20] Isaac said: "I have partaken from everything." *Genesis* 27:33
[21] Jacob said: "I have everything." *Genesis* 33:11

[the] merit	זְכוּת,
to insure peace,	שֶׁתְּהֵא לְמִשְׁמֶרֶת שָׁלוֹם,
And may we receive a blessing from Adonoy,	וְנִשָּׂא בְרָכָה מֵאֵת יְיָ,
and kindness from the God of our deliverance;	וּצְדָקָה מֵאֱלֹהֵי יִשְׁעֵנוּ.
and may we find favor and understanding	וְנִמְצָא חֵן וְשֵׂכֶל טוֹב
in the eyes of God and man.	בְּעֵינֵי אֱלֹהִים וְאָדָם:

On Shabbos say:

May the Merciful One let us inherit	הָרַחֲמָן, הוּא יַנְחִילֵנוּ
the day which will be completely Shabbos	יוֹם שֶׁכֻּלוֹ שַׁבָּת
and rest, for life everlasting.	וּמְנוּחָה, לְחַיֵּי הָעוֹלָמִים:

May the Merciful One let us inherit	הָרַחֲמָן, הוּא יַנְחִילֵנוּ
that day which is completely good.	יוֹם שֶׁכֻּלוֹ טוֹב:

May the Merciful One make us worthy	הָרַחֲמָן, הוּא יְזַכֵּנוּ
of the days of the Moshiach	לִימוֹת הַמָּשִׁיחַ
and life of the World-to-Come.	וּלְחַיֵּי הָעוֹלָם הַבָּא.
He who is a tower of deliverance	מִגְדוֹל יְשׁוּעוֹת
to His king.[22])	מַלְכּוֹ,
and shows kindness to His anointed	וְעֹשֶׂה חֶסֶד לִמְשִׁיחוֹ,
to David and his descendants forever.[23]	לְדָוִד וּלְזַרְעוֹ עַד עוֹלָם.
He Who makes peace in His high heavens	עֹשֶׂה שָׁלוֹם בִּמְרוֹמָיו,
may He make peace for us	הוּא יַעֲשֶׂה שָׁלוֹם עָלֵינוּ,
and for all Israel,	וְעַל כָּל יִשְׂרָאֵל,
and say, Amein.	וְאִמְרוּ אָמֵן:

[22] During weekdays when we feel the darkness of exile we say: "God gives deliverance to His king," thus acknowledging His preparation for the time of redemption. On Shabbos and Yom Tov which are reminiscent of the time of the Messiah, when God will be a tower of deliverance, we state it as a fact.

[23] II Samuel 22:51

Fear Adonoy, [you] His holy ones,	יְראוּ אֶת־יְיָ קְדֹשָׁיו,
for those who fear Him suffer no deprivation.	כִּי אֵין מַחְסוֹר לִירֵאָיו:
Young lions may feel want and hunger,	כְּפִירִים רָשׁוּ וְרָעֵבוּ,
but those who seek Adonoy,	וְדֹרְשֵׁי יְיָ
will not be deprived of any good thing.[24]	לֹא־יַחְסְרוּ כָל־טוֹב:
Give thanks to Adonoy, for He is good,	הוֹדוּ לַיְיָ כִּי טוֹב,
for His kindness endures forever.[25]	כִּי לְעוֹלָם חַסְדּוֹ:
You open Your hand	פּוֹתֵחַ אֶת־יָדֶךָ,
and satisfy the desire of every living being.[26]	וּמַשְׂבִּיעַ לְכָל־חַי רָצוֹן:
Blessed is the man who trusts in Adonoy,	בָּרוּךְ הַגֶּבֶר אֲשֶׁר יִבְטַח בַּיְיָ,
so that Adonoy is his security.[27]	וְהָיָה יְיָ מִבְטַחוֹ:
I was young and I have grown old,	נַעַר הָיִיתִי, גַּם זָקַנְתִּי,
yet I have never seen a righteous man forsaken,	וְלֹא רָאִיתִי צַדִּיק נֶעֱזָב,
nor his children begging for bread.[28]	וְזַרְעוֹ מְבַקֶּשׁ־לָחֶם:
Adonoy will give strength to His people,	יְיָ עֹז לְעַמּוֹ יִתֵּן,
Adonoy will bless His people with peace.[29]	יְיָ יְבָרֵךְ אֶת־עַמּוֹ בַשָּׁלוֹם:

The following blessings are said in the event you forgot to say
יַעֲלֶה וְיָבֹא *or* רְצֵה *and reminded yourself before starting the fourth*
blessing, הַטּוֹב וְהַמֵּטִיב.

If you forgot to say רְצֵה *on Shabbos:*

Blessed are You, Adonoy	בָּרוּךְ אַתָּה יְיָ,
our God, King of the Universe,	אֱלֹהֵינוּ מֶלֶךְ הָעוֹלָם,

[24] Psalms 34:10–11
[25] Psalms 136:1
[26] Psalms 145:16
[27] Jeremiah 17:7
[28] Psalms 37:25
[29] Psalms 29:11

Who gave Shabbosos for rest   אֲשֶׁר נָתַן שַׁבָּתוֹת לִמְנוּחָה

to His people Israel with love   לְעַמּוֹ יִשְׂרָאֵל בְּאַהֲבָה

for a sign and a covenant.   לְאוֹת וְלִבְרִית.

Blessed are You Adonoy,   בָּרוּךְ אַתָּה יְיָ,

Sanctifier of Shabbos.   מְקַדֵּשׁ הַשַּׁבָּת:

If you forgot to say יַעֲלֶה וְיָבֹא:

Blessed are You, Adonoy   בָּרוּךְ אַתָּה יְיָ,

our God, King of the Universe,   אֱלֹהֵינוּ מֶלֶךְ הָעוֹלָם,

Who gave Yomim Tovim   אֲשֶׁר נָתַן יָמִים טוֹבִים

to His people Israel for happiness and joy,   לְעַמּוֹ יִשְׂרָאֵל לְשָׂשׂוֹן וּלְשִׂמְחָה

this day of Pesach,   אֶת יוֹם חַג הַמַּצּוֹת הַזֶּה.

Blessed are You, Adonoy,   בָּרוּךְ אַתָּה יְיָ,

Sanctifier of Israel and the seasons.   מְקַדֵּשׁ יִשְׂרָאֵל וְהַזְּמַנִּים:

If Pesach occurs on Shabbos and you forgot to say רְצֵה *and* יַעֲלֶה וְיָבֹא:

Blessed are You, Adonoy   בָּרוּךְ אַתָּה יְיָ,

our God, King of the Universe,   אֱלֹהֵינוּ מֶלֶךְ הָעוֹלָם,

Who gave Shabbosos for rest   אֲשֶׁר נָתַן שַׁבָּתוֹת לִמְנוּחָה

to His people Israel with love,   לְעַמּוֹ יִשְׂרָאֵל בְּאַהֲבָה

for a sign and a covenant,   לְאוֹת וְלִבְרִית

and Yomim Tovim for happiness and joy,   וְיָמִים טוֹבִים לְשָׂשׂוֹן וּלְשִׂמְחָה

this day of Pesach.   אֶת יוֹם חַג הַמַּצּוֹת הַזֶּה.

Blessed are You, Adonoy,   בָּרוּךְ אַתָּה יְיָ,

Sanctifier of Shabbos, Israel,   מְקַדֵּשׁ הַשַּׁבָּת וְיִשְׂרָאֵל

and the seasons.   וְהַזְּמַנִּים:

The Third Cup   כּוֹס שְׁלִישִׁי

Everyone should lean on there left side and drink all or at least most of this third cup of wine after saying this berachah.

Blessed are You, Adonoy	בָּרוּךְ אַתָּה יְיָ,
Our God, King of the universe,	אֱלֹהֵינוּ מֶלֶךְ הָעוֹלָם,
Creator of the fruit of the vine.	בּוֹרֵא, פְּרִי הַגָּפֶן:

The cups are now filled for the fourth and concluding cup of wine. It is also customary to pour an extra cup of wine for Eliyahu, the Prophet, which has been named the כוס שֶׁל אֵלִיָהוּ the cup of Eliyahu.

It is customary to open the house door and to keep it open while reciting the following paragraph. In this prayer we ask God to destroy all godlessness and to punish the wicked and evil-doers. We also demonstrate our faith in His protection on this *Leil Shimurim,* "Night of watchfulness," by opening our doors. We trust that our faith will be rewarded with the coming of *Moshiach.* Since *Moshiach's* coming will be heralded by the Prophet Eliyahu, opening the door at this point has traditionally been associated with Eliyahu's coming.

Pour out Your wrath	שְׁפֹךְ חֲמָתְךָ
upon the nations that do not recognize You,	אֶל־הַגּוֹיִם אֲשֶׁר לֹא־יְדָעוּךָ,
and upon the kingdoms	וְעַל־מַמְלָכוֹת
that do not call upon Your Name.	אֲשֶׁר בְּשִׁמְךָ לֹא קָרָאוּ:
For they have devoured Yaakov,	כִּי אָכַל אֶת־יַעֲקֹב
and his habitation they have laid waste.	וְאֶת־נָוֵהוּ הֵשַׁמּוּ:
Pour out Your wrath upon thcm	שְׁפָךְ־עֲלֵיהֶם זַעְמֶךָ
and let Your burning wrath overtake them.	וַחֲרוֹן אַפְּךָ יַשִּׂיגֵם:
Pursue them with anger and destroy them	תִּרְדֹּף בְּאַף וְתַשְׁמִידֵם,
beneath the heavens of Adonoy.	מִתַּחַת שְׁמֵי יְיָ:

Hallel

The door is closed, and the Hallel which was begun before the meal,
is now continued:

Not for our sake, Adonoy,[30]	לֹא לָנוּ יְיָ,
not for our sake,	לֹא לָנוּ,
but unto Your Name give honor,	כִּי־לְשִׁמְךָ תֵּן כָּבוֹד.
for the sake of Your kindliness,	עַל־חַסְדְּךָ
for the sake of Your truth.	עַל־אֲמִתֶּךָ:
Why should the nations say,	לָמָּה יֹאמְרוּ הַגּוֹיִם,
"Where now is their God?"	אַיֵּה־נָא אֱלֹהֵיהֶם:
And [indeed,] our God is in heaven,	וֵאלֹהֵינוּ בַשָּׁמָיִם,
whatever He desires, He does.	כֹּל אֲשֶׁר־חָפֵץ עָשָׂה:
Their idols[31] are silver and gold,	עֲצַבֵּיהֶם כֶּסֶף וְזָהָב,
products of human hands.	מַעֲשֵׂה יְדֵי אָדָם:
They have a mouth but cannot speak,	פֶּה־לָהֶם וְלֹא יְדַבֵּרוּ,
they have eyes but cannot see,	עֵינַיִם לָהֶם וְלֹא יִרְאוּ:
they have ears but cannot hear,	אָזְנַיִם לָהֶם וְלֹא יִשְׁמָעוּ,
they have a nose, but cannot smell.	אַף לָהֶם וְלֹא יְרִיחוּן:
Their hands cannot feel.	יְדֵיהֶם וְלֹא יְמִישׁוּן,
Their feet cannot walk,	רַגְלֵיהֶם וְלֹא יְהַלֵּכוּ,
they cannot speak with their throat.	לֹא־יֶהְגּוּ בִּגְרוֹנָם:
Like them shall be their makers—	כְּמוֹהֶם יִהְיוּ עֹשֵׂיהֶם,

---

[30] According to *Seporno*, the Psalmist foresaw the destruction of the First Temple and prayed for its restoration, "not for our sake but for Your Name." He also asked God to "give honor to His Name" even during the period of exile through His performance of miracles on behalf of the righteous of the generation.

[31] עֲצַבֵּיהֶם is related to עֶצֶב which means "sadness" or "grief." *Radak* notes that idols bring only grief to those who depend on them.

all who put their trust in them.	כֹּל אֲשֶׁר־בֹּטֵחַ בָּהֶם:
Israel, trust in Adonoy;[32]	יִשְׂרָאֵל בְּטַח בַּיְיָ,
He is their help and their shield.	עֶזְרָם וּמָגִנָּם הוּא:
House of Aaron, trust in Adonoy;	בֵּית אַהֲרֹן בִּטְחוּ בַיְיָ,
He is their help and their shield.	עֶזְרָם וּמָגִנָּם הוּא:
[You] who fear Adonoy, trust in Adonoy;[33]	יִרְאֵי יְיָ בִּטְחוּ בַיְיָ,
He is their help and their shield.	עֶזְרָם וּמָגִנָּם הוּא:
Adonoy, mindful of us, will bless[34]—	יְיָ זְכָרָנוּ יְבָרֵךְ,
He will bless the House of Israel;	יְבָרֵךְ אֶת־בֵּית יִשְׂרָאֵל.
He will bless the House of Aaron.	יְבָרֵךְ אֶת־בֵּית אַהֲרֹן:
He will bless those who fear Adonoy.	יְבָרֵךְ יִרְאֵי יְיָ,
the small ones along with the great.	הַקְּטַנִּים עִם־הַגְּדֹלִים:
May Adonoy increase you,	יֹסֵף יְיָ עֲלֵיכֶם,
you and your children.[35]	עֲלֵיכֶם וְעַל־בְּנֵיכֶם:
Blessed are you unto Adonoy,	בְּרוּכִים אַתֶּם לַיְיָ,
the Maker of heaven and earth.	עֹשֵׂה שָׁמַיִם וָאָרֶץ:
The heaven is the heaven of Adonoy,[36]	הַשָּׁמַיִם שָׁמַיִם לַיְיָ,
but the earth He gave to mankind.	וְהָאָרֶץ נָתַן לִבְנֵי־אָדָם:

[32] *Maharal of Prague* notes that there are three classes of those who place their trust in God. Israel manifests their trusts in Him like children who trust in their father. The House of Aaron, those who serve God out of love, manifest trust in Him their love for Him; while those who serve God out of reverence, manifest trust in Him through their reverence for Him.

[33] The Sages say that this refers to the proselytes (who were not included in the categories previously mentioned.)

[34] The Psalmist beseeches God to bless the House of Israel each time we are mentioned before Him: "Adonoy when we are mentioned bless us."—*Maharal of Prague*

[35] He will so bless those who fear Him that the young will retain an eternal link with the old, so that the blessing of the parents will be transferred to the children.—*S.R. Hirsch*

[36] The heaven is heavenly without the efforts of man. He is not asked to perfect the heavens. The earth, however, was "given" to man as his province, and he is asked to perfect it. The earth was given to man with the injunction that he transform its material nature into a spiritual holiness dedicated to God.—*Numerous Chasidic sources*

The dead do not praise God,	לֹא־הַמֵּתִים יְהַלְלוּ־יָהּ,
nor do those who go down	וְלֹא כָּל־יֹרְדֵי
into the silence (of the grave).	דוּמָה:
But we will bless God	וַאֲנַחְנוּ נְבָרֵךְ יָהּ,
from now forever.	מֵעַתָּה וְעַד־עוֹלָם
Praise God!	הַלְלוּיָהּ:

I love when Adonoy hears[37]	אָהַבְתִּי כִּי־יִשְׁמַע יְיָ,
my voice, my prayers.	אֶת־קוֹלִי תַּחֲנוּנָי:
Because He turned His ear to me,	כִּי־הִטָּה אָזְנוֹ לִי,
throughout my days I will call [upon Him].	וּבְיָמַי אֶקְרָא:
I am encompassed with pangs of death	אֲפָפוּנִי חֶבְלֵי־מָוֶת,
and the narrow confines of the grave	וּמְצָרֵי שְׁאוֹל
come upon me;	מְצָאוּנִי,
trouble and sorrow I encounter.	צָרָה וְיָגוֹן אֶמְצָא:
And upon the Name, Adonoy, I call	וּבְשֵׁם־יְיָ אֶקְרָא,
"I beseech You, Adonoy, save my soul."	אָנָּה יְיָ מַלְּטָה נַפְשִׁי:
Gracious is Adonoy and righteous,	חַנּוּן יְיָ וְצַדִּיק,
and our God is compassionate.	וֵאלֹהֵינוּ מְרַחֵם:
Adonoy protects the simple;	שֹׁמֵר פְּתָאִים יְיָ,
I was brought low and He delivered me.	דַּלּוֹתִי וְלִי יְהוֹשִׁיעַ:
Return, my soul, to your restfulness,	שׁוּבִי נַפְשִׁי לִמְנוּחָיְכִי,
for Adonoy has rewarded you bountifully.	כִּי יְיָ גָּמַל עָלָיְכִי:
For You freed my soul from death,	כִּי חִלַּצְתָּ נַפְשִׁי מִמָּוֶת,
my eye from tears,	אֶת־עֵינִי מִן־דִּמְעָה,

[37] The Jewish people said: "Sovereign of the Universe! When am I loved by You? When You hear the sound of my prayer" (*Pesachim 118b*). One who loves another enjoys even the sound of his voice, regardless of the merit of his request. The Jew declares that he is loved when God listens even to the sound of his prayer—*Agra D'pirka*.

my foot from stumbling.	אֶת־רַגְלִי מִדֶּחִי:
I will walk before Adonoy	אֶתְהַלֵּךְ לִפְנֵי יְיָ,
in the land of the living.[38]	בְּאַרְצוֹת הַחַיִּים:
I had faith (even) when I said,	הֶאֱמַנְתִּי כִּי אֲדַבֵּר,
"I suffer greatly."	אֲנִי עָנִיתִי מְאֹד:
I said in my haste,	אֲנִי אָמַרְתִּי בְחָפְזִי,
"All men are deceitful."[39]	כָּל־הָאָדָם כֹּזֵב:
How can I repay Adonoy	מָה־אָשִׁיב לַיְיָ,
for all the rewards He bestowed on me?	כָּל־תַּגְמוּלוֹהִי עָלָי:
The cup of deliverance I will raise,[40]	כּוֹס־יְשׁוּעוֹת אֶשָּׂא,
and upon the Name, Adonoy, I will call.	וּבְשֵׁם יְיָ אֶקְרָא:
My vows to Adonoy I will fulfill	נְדָרַי לַיְיָ אֲשַׁלֵּם,
in the presence of all His people.	נֶגְדָה־נָּא לְכָל־עַמּוֹ:
Precious in the eyes of Adonoy	יָקָר בְּעֵינֵי יְיָ,
is the death of His pious ones.[41]	הַמָּוְתָה לַחֲסִידָיו:
I beseech You, Adonoy,[42]	אָנָּה יְיָ
for I am Your servant—	כִּי־אֲנִי עַבְדֶּךָ,
I am Your servant,	אֲנִי עַבְדְּךָ
the son of Your handmaid;	בֶּן־אֲמָתֶךָ,
Your have loosened my bonds.	פִּתַּחְתָּ לְמוֹסֵרָי:

---

[38] According the *Rashi* and *Radak,* the land of the living refers to Eretz Yisroel.

[39] David said this when he was forced to flee from Absalom. Others say that it refers to his troubles when Saul tried to trap him. (See *I Samuel* 23)

[40] The word יְשׁוּעוֹת is plural, indicating more than one deliverance. *Ibn Ezra* says that there are many different ways in which God delivers us. Accordingly, *S.R. Hirsch* translates, "I shall raise the cup of *deliverance's many forms* and call upon the Name Adonoy."

[41] *Ibn Ezra* maintains that the word יָקָר is to be translated קָשֶׁה difficult. He interprets: "The untimely death of His pious ones is most difficult in the sight of God."

[42] The Jew pleads with God, asking the Almighty to accept him as His servant.—*Sfas Emes*

To You I will offer offerings of thanksgiving,   לְךָ־אֶזְבַּח זֶבַח תּוֹדָה,

and upon the Name, Adonoy, I will call.   וּבְשֵׁם יְיָ אֶקְרָא:

My vows to Adonoy I will fulfill.   נְדָרַי לַיְיָ אֲשַׁלֵּם,

in the presence of all His people.   נֶגְדָה־נָּא לְכָל־עַמּוֹ:

In the courtyards of the House of God,   בְּחַצְרוֹת בֵּית יְיָ,

in Your midst, Jerusalem.   בְּתוֹכֵכִי יְרוּשָׁלָיִם,

Praise God!   הַלְלוּיָהּ:

Praise Adonoy, all nations[43]   הַלְלוּ אֶת־יְיָ כָּל־גּוֹיִם,

extol Him, all peoples.   שַׁבְּחוּהוּ כָּל־הָאֻמִּים:

For His kindness overwhelmed us,   כִּי גָבַר עָלֵינוּ חַסְדּוֹ,

and Adonoy's truth is forever.   וֶאֱמֶת־יְיָ לְעוֹלָם,

Praise God!   הַלְלוּיָהּ:

It is customary to recite the following paragraph (and also the O-NO HA-SHEM, etc.) in the same manner as in the synagogue; the Seder leader recites each line and the Seder participants respond after each line with HO-DU, etc.

Thank Adonoy for He is good.   הוֹדוּ לַיְיָ כִּי־טוֹב.

for His kindness endures forever.[44]   כִּי לְעוֹלָם חַסְדּוֹ:

Let Israel declare: יֹאמַר־נָא יִשְׂרָאֵל.

for His kindness endures forever.   כִּי לְעוֹלָם חַסְדּוֹ:

---

[43] The shortest of all Psalms, it is one of the grandest. According to commentaries it refers to the Messianic times. It restates the ultimate hope of the Jew that all children of men shall one day be united in pure worship of God.

[44] Each act of kindness that God does with the Jewish People is not of a temporary nature, lasting merely a day or a year, but its effects endure forever, as it is said: "The kindlinesses of Adonoy have not ended nor are His mercies exhausted" (*Lamentations* 3:22)–*Sfas Emes*.

Response: Thank Adonoy for He is good,
for His kindness endures forever.

הוֹדוּ לַיְיָ כִּי־טוֹב.
כִּי לְעוֹלָם חַסְדּוֹ:

Let the House of Aaron declare:
for His kindness endures forever.
Response: Thank Adonoy for He is good,
for His kindness endures forever.

יֹאמְרוּ־נָא בֵית־אַהֲרֹן.
כִּי לְעוֹלָם חַסְדּוֹ:
הוֹדוּ לַיְיָ כִּי־טוֹב.
כִּי לְעוֹלָם חַסְדּוֹ:

Let those who fear Adonoy declare:
for His kindness endures is forever.
Response: Thank Adonoy for He is good,
for His kindness endures forever.

יֹאמְרוּ־נָא יִרְאֵי יְיָ.
כִּי לְעוֹלָם חַסְדּוֹ:
הוֹדוּ לַיְיָ כִּי־טוֹב.
כִּי לְעוֹלָם חַסְדּוֹ:

From the narrowness (of distress)
I called [to] God,
He answered me
with the breadth of Divine relief.
Adonoy is with me, I will not fear,
what can man do to me?
Adonoy is with me, to help me,
and I will see my enemies' (defeat).
It is better to take refuge in Adonoy[45]
than to trust in man.
It is better to take refuge in Adonoy
than to trust in nobles.
All nations surround me;

מִן־הַמֵּצַר
קָרָאתִי יָּהּ,
עָנָנִי
בַמֶּרְחָב יָהּ:
יְיָ לִי לֹא אִירָא,
מַה־יַּעֲשֶׂה לִי אָדָם:
יְיָ לִי בְּעֹזְרָי.
וַאֲנִי אֶרְאֶה בְשֹׂנְאָי:
טוֹב לַחֲסוֹת בַּיְיָ,
מִבְּטֹחַ בָּאָדָם:
טוֹב לַחֲסוֹת בַּיְיָ.
מִבְּטֹחַ בִּנְדִיבִים:
כָּל־גּוֹיִם סְבָבוּנִי,

[45] The Psalmist declares that it is far better to rely on God even without His specific assurance of help, than to place one's trust in man, even with his promises of assistance.—*Siddur HaGra*

in Adonoy's Name, I cut them down.	בְּשֵׁם יְיָ כִּי אֲמִילַם:
They surrounded me, they surround me;	סַבּוּנִי גַם־סְבָבוּנִי,
in Adonoy's Name. I cut them down.	בְּשֵׁם יְיָ כִּי אֲמִילַם:
They surrounded me like bees,	סַבּוּנִי כִדְבֹרִים,
[but] they were extinguished like a thorn fire;	דֹּעֲכוּ כְּאֵשׁ קוֹצִים,
in Adonoy's Name, I cut them down.	בְּשֵׁם יְיָ כִּי אֲמִילַם:
You pushed me again and again[46] to fall,	דָּחֹה דְחִיתַנִי לִנְפֹּל,
but Adonoy helped me,	וַיְיָ עֲזָרָנִי:
The strength and retribution of God	עָזִּי וְזִמְרָת יָהּ,
was (the cause of) my deliverance.	וַיְהִי־לִי לִישׁוּעָה:
The sound of joyous song and deliverance	קוֹל רִנָּה וִישׁוּעָה,
is in the tents of the righteous:	בְּאָהֳלֵי צַדִּיקִים,
the right hand of Adonoy	יְמִין יְיָ
performs deeds of valor.	עֹשָׂה חָיִל:
The right hand of Adonoy is exalted,	יְמִין יְיָ רוֹמֵמָה,
the right hand of Adonoy	יְמִין יְיָ
performs deeds of valor.	עֹשָׂה חָיִל:
I shall not die; for I shall live	לֹא־אָמוּת כִּי־אֶחְיֶה,
and relate the deeds of God.	וַאֲסַפֵּר מַעֲשֵׂי יָהּ:
God has severely chastised me,	יַסֹּר יִסְּרַנִּי יָּהּ,
but unto death He has not handed me.	וְלַמָּוֶת לֹא נְתָנָנִי:
Open for me the gates of righteousness;	פִּתְחוּ־לִי שַׁעֲרֵי־צֶדֶק,
I will enter them,	אָבֹא־בָם
I will give thanks unto God.	אוֹדֶה יָהּ:
This gate is Adonoy's	זֶה־הַשַּׁעַר לַיְיָ,
the righteous shall enter it.	צַדִּיקִים יָבֹאוּ בוֹ:

---

[46] The Psalmist addresses his enemies.

I thank You for You answered me,[47]	אוֹדְךָ כִּי עֲנִיתָנִי,
and You have been my deliverance.	וַתְּהִי־לִי לִישׁוּעָה:
I thank You for You answered me,	אוֹדְךָ כִּי עֲנִיתָנִי,
and You have been my deliverance.	וַתְּהִי־לִי לִישׁוּעָה:
The stone which the builders scorned	אֶבֶן מָאֲסוּ הַבּוֹנִים,
became the cornerstone.[48]	הָיְתָה לְרֹאשׁ פִּנָּה:
The stone which the builders scorned	אֶבֶן מָאֲסוּ הַבּוֹנִים,
became the cornerstone.	הָיְתָה לְרֹאשׁ פִּנָּה:
This is Adonoy's doing,	מֵאֵת יְיָ הָיְתָה זֹּאת,
it is a marvel in our eyes.	הִיא נִפְלָאת בְּעֵינֵינוּ:
This is Adonoy's doing,	מֵאֵת יְיָ הָיְתָה זֹּאת,
it is a marvel in our eyes.	הִיא נִפְלָאת בְּעֵינֵינוּ:
This day was made by Adonoy,	זֶה־הַיּוֹם עָשָׂה יְיָ,
let us exult and rejoice in Him.	נָגִילָה וְנִשְׂמְחָה בוֹ:
This day was made by Adonoy.	זֶה־הַיּוֹם עָשָׂה יְיָ,
let us exult and rejoice in Him.	נָגִילָה וְנִשְׂמְחָה בוֹ:
We implore You, Adonoy, deliver us!	אָנָּא יְיָ הוֹשִׁיעָה נָּא:
We beseech You, Adonoy, deliver us!	אָנָּא יְיָ הוֹשִׁיעָה נָּא:
We beseech You, Adonoy, make us successful!	אָנָּא יְיָ הַצְלִיחָה נָא:
We beseech You, Adonoy, make us successful!	אָנָּא יְיָ הַצְלִיחָה נָא:
Blessed be him who comes	בָּרוּךְ הַבָּא
in the Name of Adonoy;	בְּשֵׁם יְיָ:

---

[47] According to *Sfas Emes* the word עֲנִיתָנִי can also read עִנִּיתָנִי which is translated, "You have afflicted me." The Psalmist thanks God for afflicting him, because that affliction became the source of his deliverance.

[48] According to our Sages, this verse was recited by David's father, Yishai, when the prophet, Samuel chose David as the one destined to be king of Israel. Yishai thought that one of his other sons would be selected, as he considered David to be inferior to them.

we bless you from Adonoy's House.	בֵּרַכְנוּכֶם מִבֵּית יְיָ:
Blessed be him who comes	בָּרוּךְ הַבָּא
in the Name of Adonoy;	בְּשֵׁם יְיָ,
we bless you from Adonoy's House.	בֵּרַכְנוּכֶם מִבֵּית יְיָ:

Almighty, Adonoy, He gave us light;	אֵל יְיָ וַיָּאֶר לָנוּ,
bind the festival sacrifices with ropes[49]	אִסְרוּ־חַג בַּעֲבֹתִים,
(until they are brought) to the corners	עַד־קַרְנוֹת
of the Altar.	הַמִּזְבֵּחַ:
Almighty, Adonoy, He gave us light;	אֵל יְיָ וַיָּאֶר לָנוּ,
bind the festival sacrifices with ropes	אִסְרוּ־חַג בַּעֲבֹתִים,
(untl they are brought) to the corners	עַד־קַרְנוֹת
of the Altar.	הַמִּזְבֵּחַ:

You are my Almighty	אֵלִי אַתָּה
and I will give thanks to You;	וְאוֹדֶךָּ,
My God, I will exalt You.	אֱלֹהַי אֲרוֹמְמֶךָּ:
You are my Almighty	אֵלִי אַתָּה
and I will give thanks to You;	וְאוֹדֶךָּ,
My God, I will exalt You.	אֱלֹהַי אֲרוֹמְמֶךָּ:

Thank Adonoy for He is good;	הוֹדוּ לַיְיָ כִּי־טוֹב,
for His kindness endures forever.	כִּי לְעוֹלָם חַסְדּוֹ:
Thank Adonoy for He is good;	הוֹדוּ לַיְיָ כִּי־טוֹב,
for His kindness endures forever.	כִּי לְעוֹלָם חַסְדּוֹ:

---

[49] The offerings that were brought free of blemish were tied down to protect them until they could be sacrificed and their blood sprinkled on the corners of the Altar.

Thank Adonoy for He is good,   הוֹדוּ לַייָ כִּי־טוֹב,

for His kindliness endures forever.[50]   כִּי לְעוֹלָם חַסְדּוֹ:

Thank the God of gods,   הוֹדוּ לֵאלֹהֵי הָאֱלֹהִים,

for His kindliness endures forever.   כִּי לְעוֹלָם חַסְדּוֹ:

Thank the Master of masters,   הוֹדוּ לַאֲדֹנֵי הָאֲדֹנִים,

for His kindliness endures forever.   כִּי לְעוֹלָם חַסְדּוֹ:

He Who does great wonders, alone,   לְעֹשֵׂה נִפְלָאוֹת גְּדֹלוֹת לְבַדּוֹ,

for His kindliness endures forever.   כִּי לְעוֹלָם חַסְדּוֹ:

He Who makes the heavens,   לְעֹשֵׂה הַשָּׁמַיִם

with understanding,   בִּתְבוּנָה,

for His kindliness endures forever.   כִּי לְעוֹלָם חַסְדּוֹ:

He Who spreads the earth over the waters,   לְרֹקַע הָאָרֶץ עַל־הַמָּיִם,

for His kindliness endures forever.   כִּי לְעוֹלָם חַסְדּוֹ:

He Who makes the great luminaries,   לְעֹשֵׂה אוֹרִים גְּדֹלִים,

for His kindliness endures forever,   כִּי לְעוֹלָם חַסְדּוֹ:

The sun to rule by day,   אֶת־הַשֶּׁמֶשׁ לְמֶמְשֶׁלֶת בַּיּוֹם,

for His kindliness endures forever.   כִּי לְעוֹלָם חַסְדּוֹ:

The moon and stars   אֶת־הַיָּרֵחַ וְכוֹכָבִים

to rule by night,   לְמֶמְשָׁלוֹת בַּלָּיְלָה,

for His kindliness endures forever.   כִּי לְעוֹלָם חַסְדּוֹ:

He Who struck Egypt through their firstborn,   לְמַכֵּה מִצְרַיִם בִּבְכוֹרֵיהֶם,

for His kindliness endures forever.   כִּי לְעוֹלָם חַסְדּוֹ:

He brought Israel out of their midst,   וַיּוֹצֵא יִשְׂרָאֵל מִתּוֹכָם,

for His kindliness endures forever.   כִּי לְעוֹלָם חַסְדּוֹ:

With a strong hand and outstretched arm,   בְּיָד חֲזָקָה וּבִזְרוֹעַ נְטוּיָה,

---

[50] This refrain is repeated in all twenty-six verses of the psalm. We thereby declare that each act of kindliness for which we thank God is not of a temporary nature, lasting merely a day or a year. The *effect* of His kindliness endures forever, and we continually reap the benefits of every act of Divine kindliness.

for His kindliness endures forever.   כִּי לְעוֹלָם חַסְדּוֹ:

He Who parted the Sea of Reeds into parts,[51]   לְגֹזֵר יַם־סוּף לִגְזָרִים,

for His kindliness endures forever.   כִּי לְעוֹלָם חַסְדּוֹ:

And He made Israel pass through it   וְהֶעֱבִיר יִשְׂרָאֵל בְּתוֹכוֹ,

for His kindliness endures forever.   כִּי לְעוֹלָם חַסְדּוֹ:

And He threw Pharaoh and his army
into the Sea of Reeds,   וְנִעֵר פַּרְעֹה וְחֵילוֹ
בְיַם־סוּף,

for His kindliness endures forever.   כִּי לְעוֹלָם חַסְדּוֹ:

He Who led His people through the wilderness   לְמוֹלִיךְ עַמּוֹ בַּמִּדְבָּר,

for His kindliness endures forever.   כִּי לְעוֹלָם חַסְדּוֹ:

He Who struck great kings,   לְמַכֵּה מְלָכִים גְּדֹלִים,

for His kindliness endures forever;   כִּי לְעוֹלָם חַסְדּוֹ:

and Who slew mighty kings,   וַיַּהֲרֹג מְלָכִים אַדִּירִים,

for His kindliness endures forever.   כִּי לְעוֹלָם חַסְדּוֹ:

Sichon, king of the Amorites,   לְסִיחוֹן מֶלֶךְ הָאֱמֹרִי,

for His kindliness endures forever.   כִּי לְעוֹלָם חַסְדּוֹ:

And Og, king of the Bashan,   וּלְעוֹג מֶלֶךְ הַבָּשָׁן,

for His kindliness endures forever.   כִּי לְעוֹלָם חַסְדּוֹ:

And gave their land as an inheritance,   וְנָתַן אַרְצָם לְנַחֲלָה,

for His kindliness endures forever.   כִּי לְעוֹלָם חַסְדּוֹ:

An inheritance to Israel, His servant,   נַחֲלָה לְיִשְׂרָאֵל עַבְדּוֹ,

for His kindliness endures forever.   כִּי לְעוֹלָם חַסְדּוֹ:

In our lowliness, He remembered us,   שֶׁבְּשִׁפְלֵנוּ זָכַר־לָנוּ,

for His kindliness endures forever.   כִּי לְעוֹלָם חַסְדּוֹ:

And He freed us from our oppressors,   וַיִּפְרְקֵנוּ מִצָּרֵינוּ,

for His kindliness endures forever.   כִּי לְעוֹלָם חַסְדּוֹ:

He gives food to all flesh,   נֹתֵן לֶחֶם לְכָל־בָּשָׂר,

---

[51] The sea was divided into twelve parts, so that each tribe crossed on its own route.

for His kindliness endures forever.	כִּי לְעוֹלָם חַסְדּוֹ:
Thank the Almighty of heaven	הוֹדוּ לְאֵל הַשָּׁמָיִם,
for His kindliness endures forever.[52]	כִּי לְעוֹלָם חַסְדּוֹ:

The soul of every living thing	**נִשְׁמַת** כָּל־חַי
shall bless Your Name, Adonoy, our God;	תְּבָרֵךְ אֶת־שִׁמְךָ יְיָ אֱלֹהֵינוּ.
and the spirit of all flesh	וְרוּחַ כָּל־בָּשָׂר
shall glorify and exalt	תְּפָאֵר וּתְרוֹמֵם
Your mention, our King, continually.	זִכְרְךָ מַלְכֵּנוּ תָּמִיד.
From world to world,	מִן־הָעוֹלָם וְעַד־הָעוֹלָם
You are Almighty;	אַתָּה אֵל,
and besides You	וּמִבַּלְעָדֶיךָ
we have no king, redeemer, or deliverer,	אֵין לָנוּ מֶלֶךְ גּוֹאֵל וּמוֹשִׁיעַ
[who] liberates, rescues, maintains	פּוֹדֶה וּמַצִּיל וּמְפַרְנֵס
and is compassionate	וּמְרַחֵם
in all times of trouble and distress.	בְּכָל־עֵת צָרָה וְצוּקָה.
We have no king, but You.	אֵין לָנוּ מֶלֶךְ אֶלָּא אָתָּה:
God of the first and last [generations],	אֱלֹהֵי הָרִאשׁוֹנִים וְהָאַחֲרוֹנִים
God of all created things,	אֱלוֹהַּ כָּל־בְּרִיּוֹת,
Master of all begotten things,[53]	אֲדוֹן כָּל־תּוֹלָדוֹת
Who is extolled with a multitude of praises,	הַמְהֻלָּל בְּרֹב הַתִּשְׁבָּחוֹת
Who conducts His world with kindliness	הַמְנַהֵג עוֹלָמוֹ בְּחֶסֶד

---

[52] The twenty six verses in this psalms symbolize the twenty six generations of man from Creation till the Torah was given. These generations were sustained solely by virtue of God's kindliness even though they did not have the merit of Torah.

[53] *Etz Yosef* assumes that תּוֹלָדוֹת refers to events that occur in time. [See *Proverbs* 27:1, כִּי לֹא תֵדַע מַה יֵּלֶד יוֹם, for you don't know what a day may bring forth. Thus God is *Master of all events*. *Iyun Tefiloh* says that בְּרִיּוֹת, *created beings*, refers to everything God created during the six days of creation, whereas תּוֹלָדוֹת refers to those things that come forth, i.e., were "born" from the original created things. Thus He is God of all created things and Master of all begotten things even though they appear as products of nature.

and His creatures with compassion.	בְּרִיּוֹתָיו בְּרַחֲמִים.
Adonoy neither slumbers nor sleeps.	וַיְיָ לֹא־יָנוּם וְלֹא יִישָׁן.
He arouses those who sleep	הַמְּעוֹרֵר יְשֵׁנִים
and awakens those who slumber,	וְהַמֵּקִיץ נִרְדָּמִים
and He gives speech to the mute,	וְהַמֵּשִׂיחַ אִלְּמִים
and releases the imprisoned.	וְהַמַּתִּיר אֲסוּרִים
He supports those who have fallen	וְהַסּוֹמֵךְ נוֹפְלִים
and straightens the bent.	וְהַזּוֹקֵף כְּפוּפִים
To You alone we give thanks.	וּלְךָ לְבַדְּךָ אֲנַחְנוּ מוֹדִים:
Even if our mouths were filled with song	וְאִלּוּ פִינוּ מָלֵא שִׁירָה
like the sea,[54]	כַּיָּם,
and our tongues with exultation	וּלְשׁוֹנֵנוּ רִנָּה
like the roaring of its waves,	כַּהֲמוֹן גַּלָּיו
and our lips with praise	וְשִׂפְתוֹתֵינוּ שֶׁבַח
like the breadth of the firmament,	כְּמֶרְחֲבֵי רָקִיעַ
and our eyes were radiant	וְעֵינֵינוּ מְאִירוֹת
like the sun and the moon,	כַּשֶּׁמֶשׁ וְכַיָּרֵחַ
and our hands outspread	וְיָדֵינוּ פְרוּשׂוֹת
like [the] eagles of the sky,	כְּנִשְׁרֵי שָׁמָיִם
and our feet light as the deer—	וְרַגְלֵינוּ קַלּוֹת כָּאַיָּלוֹת
we would never sufficiently	אֵין אֲנַחְנוּ מַסְפִּיקִים
thank You, Adonoy, our God	לְהוֹדוֹת לְךָ יְיָ אֱלֹהֵינוּ
and God of our fathers,	וֵאלֹהֵי אֲבוֹתֵינוּ
and bless Your Name	וּלְבָרֵךְ אֶת־שְׁמֶךָ
for even one thousandth	עַל־אַחַת מֵאָלֶף
of the billions	אֶלֶף אַלְפֵי אֲלָפִים
and trillions	וְרִבֵּי רְבָבוֹת פְּעָמִים

[54] Just like the sea is filled with water.

of favors which You did for our fathers	הַטּוֹבוֹת שֶׁעָשִׂיתָ עִם־אֲבוֹתֵינוּ
and for us:	וְעִמָּנוּ:
from Egypt You redeemed us,	מִמִּצְרַיִם גְּאַלְתָּנוּ
Adonoy, our God;	יְיָ אֱלֹהֵינוּ
from the house of bondage, You liberated us;	וּמִבֵּית עֲבָדִים פְּדִיתָנוּ.
in famine You nourished us,	בְּרָעָב זַנְתָּנוּ
and in [times of] plenty, You fed us;	וּבְשָׂבָע כִּלְכַּלְתָּנוּ
from the sword You saved us	מֵחֶרֶב הִצַּלְתָּנוּ
and from pestilence You removed us,	וּמִדֶּבֶר מִלַּטְתָּנוּ
and from severe and lingering sicknesses,	וּמֵחֳלָיִם רָעִים וְנֶאֱמָנִים
have You withdrawn us.	דִּלִּיתָנוּ:
Until now	עַד־הֵנָּה
Your compassion has helped us	עֲזָרוּנוּ רַחֲמֶיךָ,
and Your kindliness has not forsaken us.	וְלֹא־עֲזָבוּנוּ חֲסָדֶיךָ.
Do not abandon us, Adonoy, our God,	וְאַל־תִּטְּשֵׁנוּ יְיָ אֱלֹהֵינוּ
for eternity.	לָנֶצַח:
Therefore,	עַל־כֵּן
the limbs which You apportioned for us,	אֵבָרִים שֶׁפִּלַּגְתָּ בָּנוּ
and the spirit and soul	וְרוּחַ וּנְשָׁמָה
that You have breathed into our nostrils,	שֶׁנָּפַחְתָּ בְּאַפֵּינוּ
and the tongue You have set in our mouth—	וְלָשׁוֹן אֲשֶׁר שַׂמְתָּ בְּפִינוּ
behold, they will thank, bless,	הֵן הֵם יוֹדוּ וִיבָרְכוּ
praise, glorify, exalt,	וִישַׁבְּחוּ וִיפָאֲרוּ וִירוֹמְמוּ
revere, sanctify, and proclaim the sovereignty	וְיַעֲרִיצוּ וְיַקְדִּישׁוּ וְיַמְלִיכוּ
of Your Name, our King,	אֶת־שִׁמְךָ מַלְכֵּנוּ תָּמִיד:
For every mouth will thank You,	כִּי כָל־פֶּה לְךָ יוֹדֶה
and every tongue will swear allegiance to You,	וְכָל־לָשׁוֹן לְךָ תִשָּׁבַע
and every knee will bend to You,	וְכָל־בֶּרֶךְ לְךָ תִכְרַע
and all that stand up	וְכָל־קוֹמָה

will prostrate themselves before You;	לְפָנֶיךָ תִשְׁתַּחֲוֶה.
all hearts will fear You,	וְכָל־לְבָבוֹת יִירָאוּךָ
and all innards and kidneys	וְכָל־קֶרֶב וּכְלָיוֹת
will sing to Your Name	יְזַמְּרוּ לִשְׁמֶךָ
as it is written,	כַּדָּבָר שֶׁכָּתוּב
"All my bones will say:	כָּל־עַצְמוֹתַי תֹּאמַרְנָה
Adonoy! who is like unto You?"	יְיָ מִי כָמוֹךָ:
You save the poor man	מַצִּיל עָנִי
from one stronger than him,	מֵחָזָק מִמֶּנּוּ
and the poor and needy	וְעָנִי וְאֶבְיוֹן
from one who would rob him.[55]	מִגֹּזְלוֹ:
Who is like You?	מִי יִדְמֶה־לָּךְ
Who is equal to You?	וּמִי יִשְׁוֶה־לָּךְ
And who can be compared to You?	וּמִי יַעֲרָךְ־לָךְ.
The Almighty,	הָאֵל
the Great, the Powerful, the Awesome	הַגָּדוֹל הַגִּבּוֹר וְהַנּוֹרָא
most high Almighty,	אֵל עֶלְיוֹן,
Possessor of heaven and earth.	קֹנֵה שָׁמַיִם וָאָרֶץ:
We will extol You, we will praise You,	נְהַלֶּלְךָ וּנְשַׁבֵּחֲךָ
we will glorify You,	וּנְפָאֶרְךָ
and bless Your holy Name	וּנְבָרֵךְ אֶת־שֵׁם קָדְשֶׁךָ
as it is said,	כָּאָמוּר.
"By David:	לְדָוִד
My soul, bless Adonoy!	בָּרְכִי נַפְשִׁי אֶת־יְיָ
and all that is within me [bless]	וְכָל־קְרָבַי
His holy Name!"[56]	אֶת־שֵׁם קָדְשׁוֹ:

---

[55] *Psalms* 35:10.
[56] *Psalms* 103:1.

[You are] Almighty	הָאֵל
in the power of Your might;	בְּתַעֲצָמוֹת עֻזֶּךָ
Great in the honor of Your Name,	הַגָּדוֹל בִּכְבוֹד שְׁמֶךָ
Powerful for ever	הַגִּבּוֹר לָנֶצַח
and awesome through Your awesome deeds;	וְהַנּוֹרָא בְּנוֹרְאוֹתֶיךָ׃
the King Who sits on a throne	הַמֶּלֶךְ הַיּוֹשֵׁב עַל־כִּסֵּא
[that is] exalted and uplifted.	רָם וְנִשָּׂא׃

He Who dwells in eternity,	**שׁוֹכֵן־עַד**
exalted and holy is His Name.	מָרוֹם וְקָדוֹשׁ שְׁמוֹ׃
And it is written:	וְכָתוּב,
"Joyfully exult in God, [you] righteous ones,	רַנְּנוּ צַדִּיקִים בַּיְיָ
for the upright, praise is fitting.[57]	לַיְשָׁרִים נָאוָה תְהִלָּה׃
Through the mouth of the upright,	בְּפִי יְשָׁרִים
You are extolled;	תִּתְהַלָּל
and with the words of the righteous	וּבְשִׂפְתֵי צַדִּיקִים
You are blessed;	תִּתְבָּרַךְ
and by the tongue of the pious,	וּבִלְשׁוֹן חֲסִידִים
You are exalted,	תִּתְרוֹמָם
and in the midst of the holy,	וּבְקֶרֶב קְדוֹשִׁים
You are sanctified.	תִּתְקַדָּשׁ׃

And in the assemblies	**וּבְמַקְהֲלוֹת**
of myriads of Your people, the House of Israel;	רִבְבוֹת עַמְּךָ בֵּית יִשְׂרָאֵל
with joyful song	בְּרִנָּה
glorified will be Your Name, our King,	יִתְפָּאַר שִׁמְךָ מַלְכֵּנוּ
in every generation.	בְּכָל־דּוֹר וָדוֹר׃

[57] *Psalms* 33:1.

For it is the duty	שֶׁכֵּן חוֹבַת
of all beings, before You,	כָּל־הַיְצוּרִים לְפָנֶיךָ
Adonoy, our God and God of our fathers,	יְיָ אֱלֹהֵינוּ וֵאלֹהֵי אֲבוֹתֵינוּ
to thank, to extol, and to praise;	לְהוֹדוֹת לְהַלֵּל לְשַׁבֵּחַ
to glorify, to exalt, and to honor;	לְפָאֵר לְרוֹמֵם לְהַדֵּר
to bless, to elevate, and to acclaim [You,]	לְבָרֵךְ לְעַלֵּה וּלְקַלֵּס
even beyond all the words	עַל־כָּל־דִּבְרֵי
of song and praise	שִׁירוֹת וְתִשְׁבְּחוֹת
of David, son of Yishai,	דָּוִד בֶּן־יִשַׁי
Your servant, Your annointed.	עַבְדְּךָ מְשִׁיחֶךָ:

Praised be Your Name forever, our King	יִשְׁתַּבַּח שִׁמְךָ לָעַד מַלְכֵּנוּ.
Almighty the great and holy King	הָאֵל הַמֶּלֶךְ הַגָּדוֹל וְהַקָּדוֹשׁ
in heaven and on earth.	בַּשָּׁמַיִם וּבָאָרֶץ.
For to You it is fitting [to offer]	כִּי־לְךָ נָאֶה
Adonoy, our God, and God of our fathers,	יְיָ אֱלֹהֵינוּ וֵאלֹהֵי אֲבוֹתֵינוּ
song and praise, glorification and hymns,	שִׁיר וּשְׁבָחָה, הַלֵּל וְזִמְרָה,
[to proclaim your] strength and dominion,	עֹז וּמֶמְשָׁלָה,
victory, grandeur, and might,	נֶצַח גְּדֻלָּה וּגְבוּרָה,
praise and glory,	תְּהִלָּה וְתִפְאֶרֶת,
holiness and sovereignty,	קְדֻשָּׁה וּמַלְכוּת,
blessings and thanksgivings,	בְּרָכוֹת וְהוֹדָאוֹת
from now forever.	מֵעַתָּה וְעַד־עוֹלָם:

Your praise, Adonoy our God,	יְהַלְלוּךָ יְיָ אֱלֹהֵינוּ
[will be proclaimed by] all Your works,	כָּל־מַעֲשֶׂיךָ
Your pious ones, the righteous,	וַחֲסִידֶיךָ צַדִּיקִים
who do Your will;	עוֹשֵׂי רְצוֹנֶךָ.
and all Your people, the House of Israel,	וְכָל־עַמְּךָ בֵּית יִשְׂרָאֵל

will joyfully thank and bless,	בְּרִנָּה יוֹדוּ וִיבָרְכוּ
praise and glorify,	וִישַׁבְּחוּ וִיפָאֲרוּ
exalt and revere,	וִירוֹמְמוּ וְיַעֲרִיצוּ
sanctify and proclaim the sovereignty	וְיַקְדִּישׁוּ וְיַמְלִיכוּ
of Your Name, our King.	אֶת־שִׁמְךָ מַלְכֵּנוּ.
For to You it is good to give thanks,	כִּי־לְךָ טוֹב לְהוֹדוֹת
and to Your Name it is fitting to sing praises,	וּלְשִׁמְךָ נָאֶה לְזַמֵּר
for from this world to the next,	כִּי מֵעוֹלָם וְעַד־עוֹלָם
You are Almighty.	אַתָּה אֵל:
Blessed are You, Adonoy,	בָּרוּךְ אַתָּה יְיָ,
King, Who is extolled with praises.	מֶלֶךְ מְהֻלָּל בַּתִּשְׁבָּחוֹת:

The Fourth Cup   כּוֹס רְבִיעִי

After reciting the following berachah, drink the fourth cup of wine. This cup of wine too must be drunk while leaning on your left side. You must drink a full revi'is which is at least 3.3 ounces, or according to some 5.3 ounces.

Blessed are You, Adonoy,	בָּרוּךְ אַתָּה יְיָ,
our God, King of the Universe	אֱלֹהֵינוּ מֶלֶךְ הָעוֹלָם,
Creator of the fruit of the wine	בּוֹרֵא, פְּרִי הַגָּפֶן:

Recite the following concluding berachah:

Blessed are You, Adonoy,	בָּרוּךְ אַתָּה יְיָ,
our God, King of the Universe,	אֱלֹהֵינוּ מֶלֶךְ הָעוֹלָם,
for the vine and the fruit of the vine;	עַל־הַגֶּפֶן וְעַל־פְּרִי הַגֶּפֶן,
for the produce of the field;	וְעַל־תְּנוּבַת הַשָּׂדֶה,
and for the land	וְעַל־אֶרֶץ
which is delightful, good, and spacious	חֶמְדָּה טוֹבָה וּרְחָבָה,
that You were pleased	שֶׁרָצִיתָ

to allot as a heritage to our ancestors,	וְהִנְחַלְתָּ לַאֲבוֹתֵינוּ,
to eat of its fruit	לֶאֱכוֹל מִפִּרְיָהּ
and to be satisfied with its goodness.	וְלִשְׂבּוֹעַ מִטּוּבָהּ.
Have compassion Adonoy, our God,	רַחֵם נָא יְיָ אֱלֹהֵינוּ
upon Israel, Your people,	עַל־יִשְׂרָאֵל עַמֶּךָ,
upon Jerusalem, Your city,	וְעַל־יְרוּשָׁלַיִם עִירֶךָ,
upon Zion, the dwelling place of Your glory,	וְעַל־צִיּוֹן מִשְׁכַּן כְּבוֹדֶךָ,
upon Your Altar and upon Your Temple.	וְעַל־מִזְבְּחֶךָ וְעַל־הֵיכָלֶךָ.
Rebuild Jerusalem, city of the Holy Sanctuary	וּבְנֵה יְרוּשָׁלַיִם עִיר הַקֹּדֶשׁ
speedily in our days:	בִּמְהֵרָה בְיָמֵינוּ
bring us up into it	וְהַעֲלֵנוּ לְתוֹכָהּ
and cause us to rejoice in its rebuilding;	וְשַׂמְּחֵנוּ בְּבִנְיָנָהּ
let us eat from its fruit	וְנֹאכַל מִפִּרְיָהּ,
and be satisfied with its goodness,	וְנִשְׂבַּע מִטּוּבָהּ
and bless You for it	וּנְבָרֶכְךָ עָלֶיהָ
in holiness and purity.	בִּקְדֻשָּׁה וּבְטָהֳרָה:

On Shabbos add:

May it please You to strengthen us	וּרְצֵה וְהַחֲלִיצֵנוּ
on this Shabbos Day.	בְּיוֹם הַשַּׁבָּת הַזֶּה

Cause us to rejoice on:	וְשַׂמְּחֵנוּ
this Festival of Matzos.	בְּיוֹם חַג הַמַּצּוֹת הַזֶּה:
For You, Adonoy, are good	כִּי אַתָּה יְיָ טוֹב
and beneficent to all,	וּמֵטִיב לַכֹּל
and we thank You for the land	וְנוֹדֶה־לְּךָ עַל־הָאָרֶץ
and for the fruit of the vine.	וְעַל־פְּרִי הַגָּפֶן:
Blessed are You, Adonoy,	בָּרוּךְ אַתָּה יְיָ,
for the land and for the fruit of the vine.	עַל־הָאָרֶץ וְעַל־פְּרִי הַגָּפֶן:

Nirtzah נִרְצָה

The Seder service, correctly and completely performed, will be accepted by the Almighty.

With the following song the Seder is concluded in all its requirements, and the song expresses our hope to live to the day when we will actually prepare and perform the mitzvah of the Pesach offering and thus it concludes with a prayer for redemption.

Our Seder is now completed	חֲסַל סִדּוּר פֶּסַח
in accordance with its Law,	כְּהִלְכָתוֹ.
every precept and statute fulfilled.	כְּכָל מִשְׁפָּטוֹ וְחֻקָּתוֹ.
Just as we have merited to order [arrange it]	כַּאֲשֶׁר זָכִינוּ, לְסַדֵּר אוֹתוֹ,
so may we merit to perform it.	כֵּן נִזְכֶּה לַעֲשׂוֹתוֹ:
You Who are pure, dwelling on high,	זָךְ שׁוֹכֵן מְעוֹנָה.
raise up	קוֹמֵם
Your congregation that is without number.	קְהַל עֲדַת מִי מָנָה.
Soon lead the shoots of your stock	בְּקָרוֹב נַהֵל, נִטְעֵי כַנָּה
redeemed to Zion with joyous song.	פְּדוּיִים לְצִיּוֹן בְּרִנָּה:

Next year in Yerushalayim לְשָׁנָה הַבָּאָה בִּירוּשָׁלָיִם:

The Jew constantly longs for the redemption from all exile and oppression and the coming of Moshiach. Especially on the Seder night when the redemption from Egypt is celebrated, the thought of "Next year in Jerusalem" is uppermost in our mind. Both, at the beginning of the Seder, in the HO LACHMO ANYO paragraph, and here, near the conclusion of the Seder, this is fittingly stressed.

The hope, "Next year in Jerusalem," refers clearly to the Messianic time. Even in the city of Jerusalem itself, this hope is voiced. However, some add the word "HA-B'NUYO" to the sentence, thus reading: "L'SHONO HA-BO-O BI-RUSHOLAYIM HA-B'NUYO—next year in Jerusalem Rebuilt!"

The following song is sung on the first Seder night:
On the second Seder night continue at the bottom page 89.

This song lists various historical events which took place on Pesach night, each stanza ending in the refrain: "And it happened at midnight."

Among these happenings mentioned are: Avrohom's night attack against the four kings (Gen. 14:15); God's appearance in a nightly dream to Avimelech who had taken Sarah into his harem (Gen 20:3); God's appearance in a nightly dream to Lavan to warn him against harming Yaakov (Gen. 31:24); Yaakov's nightly wrestling with the angel (Gen. 32:25); the death of the Egyptian's first-born at midnight (Ex. 12:29); Sissera's defeat by Barak and Deborah (Judges 5:20); Sancheriv's defeat at the walls of Jerusalem (II Kings 19:35); Daniel's interpretation of Nebuchadnezzar's dream (Dan. 2); Balshatzar's death (Dan. 5:30); Haman's plottings and Achasveirus' sleepless night (Esth. 6:1).

And it happened at midnight   וַיְהִי בַּחֲצִי הַלַּיְלָה

Of old, You performed many miracles at night.   אָז רוֹב־נִסִּים הִפְלֵאתָ בַּלַּיְלָה.

At the beginning of the watches of this night,   בְּרֹאשׁ אַשְׁמֹרֶת זֶה הַלַּיְלָה.

to the righteous proselyte (Avrohom)   גֵּר־צֶדֶק

you gave victory   נִצַּחְתּוֹ

when you divided the night for him.   כְּנֶחֱלַק לוֹ לַיְלָה.

And it happened at midnight.   וַיְהִי בַּחֲצִי הַלַּיְלָה:

You judged the king of Gerar (Avimelech)
in a dream at night.
You struck the Aramean (Lavan) with terror
in the dark of night.
Yisroel (Yaakov) struggled with an angel.
and prevailed over him at night.
And it happened at midnight.

דַּנְתָּ מֶלֶךְ גְּרָר
בַּחֲלוֹם הַלַּיְלָה.
הִפְחַדְתָּ אֲרַמִּי
בְּאֶמֶשׁ לַיְלָה.
וַיָּשַׂר יִשְׂרָאֵל לְמַלְאָךְ
וַיּוּכַל־לוֹ לַיְלָה,
וַיְהִי בַּחֲצִי הַלַּיְלָה:

The first-born Egyptian children
You crushed at midnight.
they did not find their wealth
when they arose at night.
The battalions of Charoshes's prince (Sissera)
You swept away through the stars at night.
And it happened at midnight.

זֶרַע בְּכוֹרֵי פַתְרוֹס
מָחַצְתָּ בַּחֲצִי הַלַּיְלָה.
חֵילָם לֹא־מָצְאוּ
בְּקוּמָם בַּלַּיְלָה,
טִיסַת נְגִיד חֲרֹשֶׁת
סִלִּיתָ בְּכוֹכְבֵי לַיְלָה.
וַיְהִי בַּחֲצִי הַלַּיְלָה:

The blasphemer (Sancherev thought
to raise his hand against Jerusalem;
you caused his dead to whither by night.
the idol, Bel, and his pedestal collapsed,
in the darkness of night.
To the man of Your delight (Daniel),
the secret vision was revealed at night.
And it happened at midnight.

יָעַץ מְחָרֵף
לְנוֹפֵף אִוּוּי
הוֹבַשְׁתָּ פְגָרָיו בַּלַּיְלָה.
כָּרַע בֵּל וּמַצָּבוֹ
בְּאִישׁוֹן לַיְלָה.
לְאִישׁ חֲמוּדוֹת
נִגְלָה רָז חֲזוֹת־לַיְלָה.
וַיְהִי בַּחֲצִי הַלַּיְלָה:

He who was drunken from the sacred vessels,
(Balshatzar) was slain on that night,
He who was rescued from the lions' den
interpreted the terrifying dreams of night.

מִשְׁתַּכֵּר בִּכְלֵי קֹדֶשׁ
נֶהֱרַג בּוֹ בַּלַּיְלָה.
נוֹשַׁע מִבּוֹר אֲרָיוֹת
פּוֹתֵר בְּעֲתוּתֵי לַיְלָה.

the Agagite (Haman) cherished hatred	שׂוֹנְאָה נָטַר אֲגָגִי
and composed decrees at night.	וְכָתַב סְפָרִים בַּלַּיְלָה.
And it happened at midnight.	וַיְהִי בַּחֲצִי הַלַּיְלָה:

You initiated your triumph over him [Haman] עוֹרַרְתָּ נִצְחֲךָ עָלָיו
with the sleepness night [of Achasveirus]. בְּנֶדֶד שְׁנַת לַיְלָה.
the wine-press, You will tread פּוּרָה תִדְרוֹךְ
for those who ask the watchman, לְשׁוֹמֵר
"When will the long night [of Exile] end? מַה־מִלַּיְלָה.
He [the Almighty] will exclaim like a watchman צָרַח כַּשׁוֹמֵר
and will say, וְשָׂח
"Morning will come, and also the night[58] אָתָא בֹקֶר וְגַם לַיְלָה.
And it happened at midnight. וַיְהִי בַּחֲצִי הַלַּיְלָה:

Bring near the day [of redemption] קָרֵב יוֹם,
which is not day nor night. אֲשֶׁר הוּא לֹא־יוֹם וְלֹא לַיְלָה.
All-High! make known רָם הוֹדַע
that Yours is day and Yours is night. כִּי־לְךָ הַיּוֹם אַף לְךָ הַלַּיְלָה.
Set guards about Your city [Yerushalayim] שׁוֹמְרִים הַפְקֵד לְעִירֶךָ
all the day and all the night. כָּל־הַיּוֹם וְכָל־הַלַּיְלָה.
Make light as the day, תָּאִיר כְּאוֹר יוֹם
the darkness of the night. חֶשְׁכַת לַיְלָה.
And it happened at midnight. וַיְהִי בַּחֲצִי הַלַּיְלָה:

On the first Seder night continue on Page 93.

The following is said on the second night of Pesach.

In this song, various historical events are enumerated which took place on Pesach, each stanza ending in the refrain: "And you shall say: This is the feast of Pesach."

[58] Morning will come for the Jews and night will come for their tormentors.

Among the listings we find Avrohom's vision as to the future happenings of Pesach (Gen. 15:14); the visit of the three angels at which time matzos were served and the Pesach sacrifice was commemorated (Gen. 18:6-7); Lot's serving of matzos and the destruction of Sodom (Gen. 19:3); the death of the Egyptians' first-born and the sparing of the Jewish homes (Ex. 12); the capture of Jericho (Josh. 6); Gideon's defeat of the Midianites (Judges 7); the defeat of Sancheriv; Balshatzar's feast; Esther's three-day fast (Esth. 4:16); Haman's hanging (Esth. 7:10).

And you shall say: וּבְכֵן וַאֲמַרְתֶּם
This is the feast of Pesach זֶבַח פֶּסַח:

The strength of Your might אֹמֶץ גְּבוּרוֹתֶיךָ
wonderously demonstrated on Pesach. הִפְלֵאתָ בַּפֶּסַח.
Above all the festivals, You exalted Pesach. בְּרֹאשׁ כָּל־מוֹעֲדוֹת נִשֵּׂאתָ פֶּסַח.
to the *Ezrach* (Avrohom) You revealed גִּלִּיתָ לְאֶזְרָחִי
the midnight miracles of Pesach. חֲצוֹת לֵיל־פֶּסַח.
And you shall say this is the feast of Pesach. וַאֲמַרְתֶּם זֶבַח פֶּסַח:

You knocked at his [Avrohom's] door דְּלָתָיו דָּפַקְתָּ
in the heat of the day on Pesach; כְּחֹם הַיּוֹם בַּפֶּסַח.
he feasted angels הִסְעִיד נוֹצְצִים
with matzos on Pesach, עֻגוֹת מַצּוֹת בַּפֶּסַח.
and he ran to the cattle, וְאֶל־הַבָּקָר רָץ
so do we read about the ox on Pesach.[59] זֵכֶר לְשׁוֹר עֵרֶךְ פֶּסַח.
And you shall say this is the feast of Pesach. וַאֲמַרְתֶּם זֶבַח פֶּסַח:

[59] This is a reference to the Parshah of the Torah we read on the second day of Pesach. See Vayikrah 22:26.

His anger was aroused against the Sodomites,   זוֹעֲמוּ סְדוֹמִים

and they were consumed in fire on Pesach;   וְלוֹהֲטוּ בָּאֵשׁ בַּפֶּסַח.

Lot was saved from among them   חֻלַּץ לוֹט מֵהֶם

and baked matzos [for the angels]   וּמַצּוֹת אָפָה

at the beginning of Pesach.   בְּקֵץ פֶּסַח.

You swept clean the land of Moph and Noph[60]   טֵאטֵאתָ אַדְמַת מוֹף וְנוֹף

when you passed through them on Pesach.   בְּעָבְרְךָ בַּפֶּסַח.

And you shall say this is the feast of Pesach.   וַאֲמַרְתֶּם זֶבַח פֶּסַח:

You, God,   יָהּ,

smote the head of every first- born   רֹאשׁ כָּל־אוֹן מָחַצְתָּ

on the watchful night of Pesach.   בְּלֵיל שִׁמּוּר פֶּסַח.

Mighty One!   כַּבִּיר

You passed over Your first-born [Israel]   עַל־בֵּן בְּכוֹר פָּסַחְתָּ

because of the blood of the Pesach offering,   בְּדַם פֶּסַח.

not allowing the destroyer [angel of death]   לְבִלְתִּי תֵת מַשְׁחִית

to enter my doors on Pesach.   לָבֹא בִּפְתָחַי בַּפֶּסַח.

And you shall say this is the feast of Pesach.   וַאֲמַרְתֶּם זֶבַח פֶּסַח:

The closed [walled city of Jericho]   מְסֻגֶּרֶת

was besieged at the time of Pesach.   סֻגְּרָה בְּעִתּוֹתֵי פֶּסַח.

Midian was destroyed by a cake of barley,[61]   נִשְׁמְדָה מִדְיָן בִּצְלִיל שְׂעוֹרֵי

the offering of the Omer on Pesach   עֹמֶר פֶּסַח.

the mighty ones of Pul and Lud were burned[62]   שׂרְפוּ מִשְׁמַנֵּי פוּל וְלוּד

---

[60] These were Egyptian provinces.

[61] See Shoftim 7:13 and Rashi's commentary.

[62] This is a reference to Sancherev's army that was destroyed on Pesach. See Yeshayahu 66:19, II Melachim 19.

in a fierce conflagration on Pesach.   בִּיקַר יְקוֹד פֶּסַח.

And you shall say this is the feast of Pesach.   וַאֲמַרְתֶּם זֶבַח פֶּסַח:

He intended to be in Nov that day[63]   עוֹד הַיּוֹם בְּנוֹב לַעֲמֹד

until there came the time of Pesach.   עַד גָּעָה עוֹנַת פֶּסַח.

An invisible hand wrote [on a wall]   פַּס יָד כָּתְבָה

the fate of Tzul [Babylon] on Pesach;   לְקַעֲקֵעַ צוּל בַּפֶּסַח.

just when the lookouts were set,   צָפֹה הַצָּפִית

and the table was spread on Pesach.   עָרוֹךְ הַשֻּׁלְחָן בַּפֶּסַח.

And you shall say this is the feast of Pesach.   וַאֲמַרְתֶּם זֶבַח פֶּסַח:

Hadassah (Esther) gathered the congregation [of Israel]   קָהָל כִּנְּסָה הֲדַסָּה

for a three day fast on Pesach.   צוֹם לְשַׁלֵּשׁ בַּפֶּסַח.

The head of the evil house (Haman)   רֹאשׁ מִבֵּית רָשָׁע

You caused to be hung   מָחַצְתָּ

on a tree fifty *amohs* high, on Pesach.   בְּעֵץ חֲמִשִּׁים בַּפֶּסַח.

These two curses[64] may You bring in a moment   שְׁתֵּי אֵלֶּה רֶגַע תָּבִיא

upon Utsis (Edom) on Pesach.   לְעוּצִית בַּפֶּסַח.

May Your hand be strong,   תָּעֹז יָדְךָ

and Your right arm uplifted, as on the night[65]   וְתָרוֹם יְמִינְךָ כְּלֵיל

of the sanctification of the festival of Pesach.   הִתְקַדֵּשׁ חַג פֶּסַח.

And you shall say this is the feast of Pesach.   וַאֲמַרְתֶּם זֶבַח פֶּסַח:

---

[63] A referene to Sancherev's advance on Nov when he threatened to capture Yerushalayim the next day, but was destroyed.

[64] Widowhood and childlessness. See Yeshayahu 47:9.

[65] May You take our revenge from our enemies and redeem us as You avenged the Bnei Yisroel and redeemed them from Egypt on the night of Pesach.

For to Him praise is proper כִּי לוֹ נָאֶה.
for to Him praise is fitting כִּי לוֹ יָאֶה:

Mighty in Kingship, truly distinguished; אַדִּיר בִּמְלוּכָה. בָּחוּר כַּהֲלָכָה.
His angelic hosts proclaim to Him: גְּדוּדָיו יֹאמְרוּ לוֹ.
Yours indeed; Yours, only Yours, לְךָ וּלְךָ. לְךָ כִּי לְךָ.
Yours surely Yours, לְךָ אַף לְךָ.
Yours, Adonoy is the sovereignity. לְךָ יְיָ הַמַּמְלָכָה.
For to Him praise is proper כִּי לוֹ נָאֶה.
for to Him praise is fitting כִּי לוֹ יָאֶה:

Pre-eminent in Kingship, truly glorious; דָּגוּל בִּמְלוּכָה. הָדוּר כַּהֲלָכָה.
His faithful proclaim to Him: וָתִיקָיו יֹאמְרוּ לוֹ.
Yours, etc. לְךָ, וכו':

Just in Kingship, truly powerful; זַכַּאי בִּמְלוּכָה. חָסִין כַּהֲלָכָה.
His angels proclaim to Him: טַפְסְרָיו יֹאמְרוּ לוֹ.
Yours, etc. לְךָ, וכו':

Unique in Kingship, truly grand; יָחִיד בִּמְלוּכָה. כַּבִּיר כַּהֲלָכָה.
His disciples proclaim to Him: לִמּוּדָיו יֹאמְרוּ לוֹ.
Yours, etc. לְךָ, וכו':

Ruler in Kingship, truly awesome; מוֹשֵׁל בִּמְלוּכָה. נוֹרָא כַּהֲלָכָה.
His surrounding angels proclaim to Him: סְבִיבָיו יֹאמְרוּ לוֹ.
Yours, etc. לְךָ, וכו':

Modest in Kingship, truly the Redeemer; עָנָיו בִּמְלוּכָה. פּוֹדֶה כַּהֲלָכָה.
His righteous ones Proclaim to Him: צַדִּיקָיו יֹאמְרוּ לוֹ.
Yours, etc. לְךָ, וכו':

Holy in Kingship, truly merciful; קָדוֹשׁ בִּמְלוּכָה. רַחוּם כַּהֲלָכָה.

His angels proclaim to Him: שִׁנְאַנָּיו יֹאמְרוּ לוֹ.

Yours, etc. לְךָ, וכו':

Resolute in Kingship, truly supportive; תַּקִּיף בִּמְלוּכָה. תּוֹמֵךְ כַּהֲלָכָה.

His perfect ones proclaim to Him תְּמִימָיו יֹאמְרוּ לוֹ.

Yours, etc. לְךָ, וכו':

He is mighty אַדִּיר הוּא.

He is mighty אַדִּיר הוּא.

May He rebuild His House soon! יִבְנֶה בֵיתוֹ בְּקָרוֹב.

Quickly, quickly, in our days soon. בִּמְהֵרָה בִּמְהֵרָה, בְּיָמֵינוּ בְּקָרוֹב.

Almighty build, Almighty build. אֵל בְּנֵה, אֵל בְּנֵה.

Rebuild Your House soon. בְּנֵה בֵיתְךָ בְּקָרוֹב:

Chosen is He, great is He, pre-eminent is He; בָּחוּר הוּא. גָּדוֹל הוּא. דָּגוּל הוּא.

May He rebuild His House soon! יִבְנֶה בֵיתוֹ בְּקָרוֹב.

Glorious is He, distinguished is He הָדוּר הוּא. וָתִיק הוּא.

Faultless is He, benevolent is He; זַכַּאי הוּא. חָסִיד הוּא.

May He rebuild His House soon! יִבְנֶה בֵיתוֹ בְּקָרוֹב.

Pure is He, unique is He, טָהוֹר הוּא. יָחִיד הוּא.

Powerful is He, all Knowing is He, כַּבִּיר הוּא. לָמוּד הוּא.

Eternal King is He, awesome is He מֶלֶךְ הוּא. נוֹרָא הוּא.

Exalted is He, invincible is He, סַגִּיב הוּא. עִזּוּז הוּא.

The redeemer is He, righteous is He; פּוֹדֶה הוּא. צַדִּיק הוּא.

May He rebuild His House soon! יִבְנֶה בֵיתוֹ בְּקָרוֹב.

Holy is He, merciful is He,   קָדוֹשׁ הוּא. רַחוּם הוּא.

Almighty is He, forceful is He,   שַׁדַּי הוּא. תַּקִּיף הוּא.

May He rebuild His House soon!   יִבְנֶה בֵיתוֹ בְּקָרוֹב.

Quickly, quickly, in our days soon.   בִּמְהֵרָה בִּמְהֵרָה, בְּיָמֵינוּ בְּקָרוֹב.

Almighty build, Almighty build   אֵל בְּנֵה. אֵל בְּנֵה.

Rebuild Your House soon.   בְּנֵה בֵיתְךָ בְּקָרוֹב:

Who knows one?   אֶחָד מִי יוֹדֵעַ?

Who knows one? I know one.   אֶחָד מִי יוֹדֵעַ? אֶחָד אֲנִי יוֹדֵעַ.

One is our God in heaven and on earth.   אֶחָד אֱלֹהֵינוּ שֶׁבַּשָּׁמַיִם וּבָאָרֶץ:

Who knows two? I know two.   שְׁנַיִם מִי יוֹדֵעַ? שְׁנַיִם אֲנִי יוֹדֵעַ.

Two are the Tablets of the Covenant.   שְׁנֵי לָחוֹת הַבְּרִית.

One is our God in heaven and on earth.   אֶחָד אֱלֹהֵינוּ שֶׁבַּשָּׁמַיִם וּבָאָרֶץ:

Who knows three?   שְׁלֹשָׁה מִי יוֹדֵעַ?

I know three.   שְׁלֹשָׁה אֲנִי יוֹדֵעַ.

Three are our Patriarchs.   שְׁלֹשָׁה אָבוֹת.

Two are the Tablets of the Covenant.   שְׁנֵי לָחוֹת הַבְּרִית.

One is our God in heaven and on earth.   אֶחָד אֱלֹהֵינוּ שֶׁבַּשָּׁמַיִם וּבָאָרֶץ:

Who knows four?   אַרְבַּע מִי יוֹדֵעַ?

I know four   אַרְבַּע אֲנִי יוֹדֵעַ.

Four are our Matriarchs.   אַרְבַּע אִמָּהוֹת.

Three are our Patriarchs,   שְׁלֹשָׁה אָבוֹת.

Two are the Tablets of the Covenant.   שְׁנֵי לָחוֹת הַבְּרִית.

One is our God in heaven and on earth.   אֶחָד אֱלֹהֵינוּ שֶׁבַּשָּׁמַיִם וּבָאָרֶץ:

Who knows five?   חֲמִשָּׁה מִי יוֹדֵעַ?

I know five.   חֲמִשָּׁה אֲנִי יוֹדֵעַ.

Five are the books of the Torah.   חֲמִשָּׁה חוּמְשֵׁי תוֹרָה.

Four are our Matriarchs. אַרְבַּע אִמָּהוֹת.
Three are our Patriarchs. שְׁלֹשָׁה אָבוֹת.
Two are the Tablets of the Covenant. שְׁנֵי לֻחוֹת הַבְּרִית.
One is our God in heaven and on earth. אֶחָד אֱלֹהֵינוּ שֶׁבַּשָּׁמַיִם וּבָאָרֶץ:

Who knows six? I know six. שִׁשָּׁה מִי יוֹדֵעַ? שִׁשָּׁה אֲנִי יוֹדֵעַ.
Six are the orders of the Mishnah. שִׁשָּׁה סִדְרֵי מִשְׁנָה.
Five are the books of the Torah. חֲמִשָּׁה חוּמְשֵׁי תוֹרָה.
Four are our Matriarchs. אַרְבַּע אִמָּהוֹת.
Three are our Patriarchs. שְׁלֹשָׁה אָבוֹת.
Two are the Tablets of the Covenant. שְׁנֵי לֻחוֹת הַבְּרִית.
One is our God in heaven and on earth. אֶחָד אֱלֹהֵינוּ שֶׁבַּשָּׁמַיִם וּבָאָרֶץ:

Who knows seven? שִׁבְעָה מִי יוֹדֵעַ?
I know seven. שִׁבְעָה אֲנִי יוֹדֵעַ.
Seven are the days of the week. שִׁבְעָה יְמֵי שַׁבַּתָּא.
Six are the orders of the Mishnah. שִׁשָּׁה סִדְרֵי מִשְׁנָה.
Five are the books of the Torah. חֲמִשָּׁה חוּמְשֵׁי תוֹרָה.
Four are our Matriarchs. אַרְבַּע אִמָּהוֹת.
Three are our Patriarchs. שְׁלֹשָׁה אָבוֹת.
Two are the Tablets of the Covenant שְׁנֵי לֻחוֹת הַבְּרִית.
One is our God in heaven and on earth. אֶחָד אֱלֹהֵינוּ שֶׁבַּשָּׁמַיִם וּבָאָרֶץ:

Who knows eight? שְׁמוֹנָה מִי יוֹדֵעַ?
I know eight. שְׁמוֹנָה אֲנִי יוֹדֵעַ.
Eight are the days for circumcision. שְׁמוֹנָה יְמֵי מִילָה.
Seven are the days of the week. שִׁבְעָה יְמֵי שַׁבַּתָּא.
Six are the orders of the Mishnah. שִׁשָּׁה סִדְרֵי מִשְׁנָה.
Five are the books of the Torah. חֲמִשָּׁה חוּמְשֵׁי תוֹרָה.
Four are our Matriarchs. אַרְבַּע אִמָּהוֹת.
Three are our Patriarchs. שְׁלֹשָׁה אָבוֹת.

Two are the Tablets of the Covenant.	שְׁנֵי לֻחוֹת הַבְּרִית.
One is our God in heaven and on earth.	אֶחָד אֱלֹהֵינוּ שֶׁבַּשָּׁמַיִם וּבָאָרֶץ:
Who knows nine?	תִּשְׁעָה מִי יוֹדֵעַ?
I know nine.	תִּשְׁעָה אֲנִי יוֹדֵעַ.
Nine are the months to childbirth.	תִּשְׁעָה יַרְחֵי לֵדָה.
Eight are the days for circumcision.	שְׁמוֹנָה יְמֵי מִילָה.
Seven are the days of the week.	שִׁבְעָה יְמֵי שַׁבַּתָּא.
Six are the orders of the Mishnah.	שִׁשָּׁה סִדְרֵי מִשְׁנָה.
Five are the books of the Torah.	חֲמִשָּׁה חוּמְשֵׁי תוֹרָה.
Four are our Matriarchs.	אַרְבַּע אִמָּהוֹת.
Three are our Partiarchs.	שְׁלֹשָׁה אָבוֹת.
Two are the Tablets of the Covenant.	שְׁנֵי לֻחוֹת הַבְּרִית.
One is our God in heaven and on earth.	אֶחָד אֱלֹהֵינוּ שֶׁבַּשָּׁמַיִם וּבָאָרֶץ:
Who knows ten?	עֲשָׂרָה מִי יוֹדֵעַ?
I know ten.	עֲשָׂרָה אֲנִי יוֹדֵעַ.
Ten are the commandments given at Sinai.	עֲשָׂרָה דִּבְּרַיָּא.
Nine are the months to childbirth.	תִּשְׁעָה יַרְחֵי לֵדָה.
Eight are the days for circumcision.	שְׁמוֹנָה יְמֵי מִילָה.
Seven are the days of the week.	שִׁבְעָה יְמֵי שַׁבַּתָּא.
Six are the orders of the Mishnah.	שִׁשָּׁה סִדְרֵי מִשְׁנָה.
Five are the books of the Torah.	חֲמִשָּׁה חוּמְשֵׁי תוֹרָה.
Four are our Matriarchs.	אַרְבַּע אִמָּהוֹת.
Three are our Patriarchs.	שְׁלֹשָׁה אָבוֹת.
Two are the Tablets of the Covenant.	שְׁנֵי לֻחוֹת הַבְּרִית.
One is our God in heaven and on earth.	אֶחָד אֱלֹהֵינוּ שֶׁבַּשָּׁמַיִם וּבָאָרֶץ:
Who knows eleven?	אַחַד עָשָׂר מִי יוֹדֵעַ?
I know eleven	אַחַד עָשָׂר אֲנִי יוֹדֵעַ.
Eleven are the stars in Joseph's dream.	אַחַד עָשָׂר כּוֹכְבַיָּא.

Ten are the commandments given at Sinai.	עֲשָׂרָה דִבְּרַיָּא.
Nine are the months to childbirth.	תִּשְׁעָה יַרְחֵי לֵדָה.
Eight are the days for circumcision.	שְׁמוֹנָה יְמֵי מִילָה.
Seven are the days of the week.	שִׁבְעָה יְמֵי שַׁבַּתָּא.
Six are the orders of the Mishnah.	שִׁשָּׁה סִדְרֵי מִשְׁנָה.
Five are the books of the Torah.	חֲמִשָּׁה חוּמְשֵׁי תוֹרָה.
Four are our Matriarchs.	אַרְבַּע אִמָּהוֹת.
Three are our Patriarchs.	שְׁלֹשָׁה אָבוֹת.
Two are the Tablets of the Covenant.	שְׁנֵי לֻחוֹת הַבְּרִית.
One is our God in heaven an on earth.	אֶחָד אֱלֹהֵינוּ שֶׁבַּשָּׁמַיִם וּבָאָרֶץ:

Who knows twelve?	שְׁנֵים עָשָׂר מִי יוֹדֵעַ?
I know twelve.	שְׁנֵים עָשָׂר אֲנִי יוֹדֵעַ.
Twelve are the Tribes of Israel.	שְׁנֵים עָשָׂר שִׁבְטַיָּא.
Eleven are the stars in Joseph's dream.	אַחַד עָשָׂר כּוֹכְבַיָּא.
Ten are the commandments given at Sinai.	עֲשָׂרָה דִבְּרַיָּא.
Nine are the months to childbirth,	תִּשְׁעָה יַרְחֵי לֵדָה.
Eight are the days for circumcision.	שְׁמוֹנָה יְמֵי מִילָה.
Seven are the days of the week.	שִׁבְעָה יְמֵי שַׁבַּתָּא.
Six are the orders of the Mishnah.	שִׁשָּׁה סִדְרֵי מִשְׁנָה.
Five are the book of the Torah.	חֲמִשָּׁה חוּמְשֵׁי תוֹרָה.
Four are our Matriarchs.	אַרְבַּע אִמָּהוֹת.
Three are our Patriarchs.	שְׁלֹשָׁה אָבוֹת.
Two are the Tablets of the Covenant.	שְׁנֵי לֻחוֹת הַבְּרִית.
One is our God in heaven and on earth.	אֶחָד אֱלֹהֵינוּ שֶׁבַּשָּׁמַיִם וּבָאָרֶץ:

Who knows thirteen?	שְׁלֹשָׁה עָשָׂר מִי יוֹדֵעַ?
I know thirteen.	שְׁלֹשָׁה עָשָׂר אֲנִי יוֹדֵעַ.
Thirteen are the attributes of God.	שְׁלֹשָׁה עָשָׂר מִדַּיָּא.
Twelve are the Tribes of Israel	שְׁנֵים עָשָׂר שִׁבְטַיָּא.

Eleven are the stars in Joseph's dream.	אַחַד עָשָׂר כּוֹכְבַיָּא.
Ten are the commandments given at Sinai.	עֲשָׂרָה דִבְּרַיָּא.
Nine are the months to childbirth.	תִּשְׁעָה יַרְחֵי לֵדָה.
Eight are the days for circumcision.	שְׁמוֹנָה יְמֵי מִילָה.
Seven are the days of the week.	שִׁבְעָה יְמֵי שַׁבַּתָּא.
Six are the orders of the Mishnah.	שִׁשָּׁה סִדְרֵי מִשְׁנָה.
Five are the books of the Torah.	חֲמִשָּׁה חוּמְשֵׁי תוֹרָה.
Four are our Matriarchs.	אַרְבַּע אִמָּהוֹת.
Three are our Patriarchs.	שְׁלֹשָׁה אָבוֹת.
Two are the Tablets of the Covenant.	שְׁנֵי לֻחוֹת הַבְּרִית.
One is our God in heaven and on earth.	אֶחָד אֱלֹהֵינוּ שֶׁבַּשָּׁמַיִם וּבָאָרֶץ:

An only kid .חַד גַּדְיָא

This popular song with which the Seder ends, tells a delightful story of a goat, This goat is bought by the father and then devoured by a cat, the cat was bitten to death by a dog, the dog was slain by a stick, the stick was consumed by fire, the fire was extinguished by water, the water was drunk by an ox, the ox was slaughtered by the Shochet, the Shochet's life was taken by the Angel of Death and finally the Angel of Death is killed by God.

Various opinions exist regarding this song. It is not simply a playful story for children but rather a song with deep meaning. The Jewish people are compared to an innocent lamb which is set upon by many enemies who devour each other in turn, until finally, God does away with all of them. Mainly the song demonstrates the justice of God, how in a long chain of natural events God's righteous retribution is clearly manifested.

An only kid, and only kid,	חַד גַּדְיָא, חַד גַּדְיָא.
Which my father bought for two zuzim;	דְּזַבִּין אַבָּא בִּתְרֵי זוּזֵי.
an only kid, an only kid.	חַד גַּדְיָא, חַד גַּדְיָא:

There came a cat and ate the kid
which my father bought for two zuzim;
an only kid, an only kid.

וְאָתָא שׁוּנְרָא. וְאָכְלָה לְגַדְיָא.
דְּזַבִּין אַבָּא בִּתְרֵי זוּזֵי.
חַד גַּדְיָא. חַד גַּדְיָא:

There came a dog and bit the cat
that ate the kid
which my father bought for two zuzim;
an only kid, an only kid.

וְאָתָא כַלְבָּא וְנָשַׁךְ לְשׁוּנְרָא.
דְּאָכְלָה לְגַדְיָא.
דְּזַבִּין אַבָּא בִּתְרֵי זוּזֵי.
חַד גַּדְיָא. חַד גַּדְיָא:

There came a stick and beat the dog
that bit the cat that ate the kid
which my father bought for two zuzim;
an only kid, an only kid.

וְאָתָא חוּטְרָא. וְהִכָּה לְכַלְבָּא
דְּנָשַׁךְ לְשׁוּנְרָא. דְּאָכְלָה לְגַדְיָא.
דְּזַבִּין אַבָּא בִּתְרֵי זוּזֵי.
חַד גַּדְיָא. חַד גַּדְיָא:

There came a fire and burnt the stick
that beat the dog that bit the cat
that ate the kid
which my father bought for two zuzim;
an only kid, an only kid.

וְאָתָא נוּרָא. וְשָׂרַף לְחוּטְרָא.
דְּהִכָּה לְכַלְבָּא דְּנָשַׁךְ לְשׁוּנְרָא.
דְּאָכְלָה לְגַדְיָא.
דְּזַבִּין אַבָּא בִּתְרֵי זוּזֵי.
חַד גַּדְיָא. חַד גַּדְיָא:

There came water and put out the fire
that burnt the stick that hit the dog
that bit the cat that ate the kid
which my father bought for two zuzim;
an only kid, an only kid.

וְאָתָא מַיָּא. וְכָבָה לְנוּרָא.
דְּשָׂרַף לְחוּטְרָא. דְּהִכָּה לְכַלְבָּא.
דְּנָשַׁךְ לְשׁוּנְרָא. דְּאָכְלָה לְגַדְיָא.
דְּזַבִּין אַבָּא בִּתְרֵי זוּזֵי.
חַד גַּדְיָא. חַד גַּדְיָא:

There came an ox and drank the water
that put out the fire that burnt the stick
that hit the dog that bit the cat
that ate the kid

וְאָתָא תוֹרָא. וְשָׁתָה לְמַיָּא.
דְּכָבָה לְנוּרָא. דְּשָׂרַף לְחוּטְרָא.
דְּהִכָּה לְכַלְבָּא. דְּנָשַׁךְ לְשׁוּנְרָא.
דְּאָכְלָה לְגַדְיָא.

which my father bought for two zuzim;	דְּזַבִּין אַבָּא בִּתְרֵי זוּזֵי.
an only kid, an only kid.	חַד גַּדְיָא. חַד גַּדְיָא:
There came a *Shochet* (slaughterer)	וְאָתָא הַשּׁוֹחֵט.
and slaughtered the ox	וְשָׁחַט לְתוֹרָא.
that drank the water that put out the fire	דְּשָׁתָה לְמַיָּא. דְּכָבָה לְנוּרָא.
that burnt the stick that hit the dog	דְּשָׂרַף לְחוּטְרָא. דְּהִכָּה לְכַלְבָּא.
that bit the cat that ate the kid	דְּנָשַׁךְ לְשׁוּנְרָא. דְּאָכְלָה לְגַדְיָא.
which my father bought for two zuzim;	דְּזַבִּין אַבָּא בִּתְרֵי זוּזֵי.
an only kid, an only kid.	חַד גַּדְיָא. חַד גַּדְיָא:
There came the angel of death	וְאָתָא מַלְאַךְ הַמָּוֶת.
and killed the slaughterer	וְשָׁחַט לְשׁוֹחֵט
who slaughtered the ox	דְּשָׁחַט לְתוֹרָא.
that drank the water that put out the fire	דְּשָׁתָה לְמַיָּא. דְּכָבָה לְנוּרָא.
that burnt the stick that hit the dog	דְּשָׂרַף לְחוּטְרָא. דְּהִכָּה לְכַלְבָּא.
that bit the cat that ate the kid	דְּנָשַׁךְ לְשׁוּנְרָא. דְּאָכְלָה לְגַדְיָא.
which my father bought for two zuzim;	דְּזַבִּין אַבָּא בִּתְרֵי זוּזֵי.
an only kid, an only kid.	חַד גַּדְיָא. חַד גַּדְיָא:
There came the Holy One blessed is He,	וְאָתָא הַקָּדוֹשׁ בָּרוּךְ הוּא.
and slaughtered the angel of death	וְשָׁחַט לְמַלְאַךְ הַמָּוֶת.
who killed the slaughterer	דְּשָׁחַט לְשׁוֹחֵט.
who slaughtered the ox	דְּשָׁחַט לְתוֹרָא.
that drank the water that put out the fire	דְּשָׁתָה לְמַיָּא. דְּכָבָה לְנוּרָא,
that burnt the stick that hit the dog	דְּשָׂרַף לְחוּטְרָא. דְּהִכָּה לְכַלְבָּא.
that bit the cat that ate the kid	דְּנָשַׁךְ לְשׁוּנְרָא. דְּאָכְלָה לְגַדְיָא.
which my father bought for two zuzim;	דְּזַבִּין אַבָּא בִּתְרֵי זוּזֵי.
an only kid, an only kid.	חַד גַּדְיָא. חַד גַּדְיָא:

The laws pertaining to Pesach (Passover) eve and the order of the *seder* (laws and rituals of the first night).

MISHNAH 1

Every Pesach Eve[1]	(א) עַרְבֵי פְּסָחִים
near the time of the *mincha* prayer,[2]	סָמוּךְ לַמִּנְחָה,
a person should not eat[3]	לֹא יֹאכַל אָדָם
until it gets dark.	עַד־שֶׁתֶּחְשַׁךְ.
And even the poorest of Jews	וַאֲפִלּוּ עָנִי שֶׁבְּיִשְׂרָאֵל
should not eat[4] without reclining.[5]	לֹא יֹאכַל עַד־שֶׁיָּסֵב.
And they[6] should [give him] not less	וְלֹא יִפְחֲתוּ לוֹ
than four cups of wine,[7]	מֵאַרְבַּע כּוֹסוֹת שֶׁל־יַיִן,
even from the poor-dish.[8]	וַאֲפִלּוּ מִן־הַתַּמְחוּי:

[1] I.e. on the day before Pesach (Passover).

[2] The *mincha* prayer corresponds to the time of the תָּמִיד שֶׁל בֵּין הָעַרְבַּיִם—the daily afternoon *korban*-sacrifice. Usually this *korban* was brought nine and one half hours into the day, i.e. the daylight hours are divided into twelve equal parts, at nine and one half of these parts the תָּמִיד שֶׁל בֵּין הָעַרְבַּיִם was brought (v. *Pesachim* chapter 5, *mishnah* 1). "Near the time of *mincha*" is approximately one half hour before this, i.e. the beginning of the tenth hour.

[3] One should not have a meal from this time on so that he may eat the *matzoh* in the evening with appetite. One may, however, have just a snack.

[4] At the *seder* on the night of Pesach.

[5] We recline during the *seder* meal to show our status as free people. Even one who is abysmally poor should recline to symbolize his freedom.

[6] Those appointed to dispense charity.

[7] The Sages decreed the *mitzvah* of "four cups" to symbolize the four terms for freedom that are found in the *Torah*. They are to be drunk: 1) at *kiddush*, 2) at the completion of the *haggadah*, 3) at *bircas hamazon*—grace after the meal, and 4) at the completion of *hallel*.

[8] I.e. even if he is so poor that he receives his food from the common dish used to distribute food to the poor.

MISHNAH 2

[When] they have poured for him[1]	(ב) מָזְגוּ־לוֹ
the first cup,	כּוֹס רִאשׁוֹן,
Beth Shammai say:	בֵּית־שַׁמַּי אוֹמְרִים,
he [first] makes the brocho	מְבָרֵךְ
on the day[2]	עַל הַיּוֹם
and afterwards he makes the brocho	וְאַחַר־כָּךְ מְבָרֵךְ
on the wine.	עַל הַיָּיִן.
But Beth Hillel say:	וּבֵית הִלֵּל אוֹמְרִים,
he [first] makes the brocho	מְבָרֵךְ
on the wine	עַל הַיַּיִן
and afterwards he makes the brocho	וְאַחַר־כָּךְ מְבָרֵךְ
on the day.[3]	עַל הַיּוֹם:

MISHNAH 3

They brought before him[1] [vegetables][2]	(ג) הֵבִיאוּ לְפָנָיו

[1] I.e. for the head of the household. To symbolize his freedom, he has others fill his cup for him.

[2] I.e. he makes the blessing of kiddush.

[3] Beth Hillel reverse the order of Beth Shammai. Beth Shammai hold that "the day," i.e. the Holiday, is what brings about the need to have wine. The day is foremost and, therefore, comes first. Secondly, the Holiday arrives before the kiddush is to be recited and, therefore, should be acknowledged first. Beth Hillel's opinion is that since wine is a prerequisite to kiddush, therefore, the brocho on the wine is recited first. Secondly, wine is drunk more often than kiddush, therefore, the wine comes before based on the rule "תָּדִיר וְשֶׁאֵינוֹ תָּדִיר, תָּדִיר קוֹדֵם" (ברכות נא, א) [when faced with a choice between two things: "One that comes often and one that does not come often, that which is often comes first."]

[1] I.e. the head of the household.

[2] Some versions of the text read: "vegetables." According to others it was the custom of the times that each participant in a meal had his own small table with the food on it before him. Here the Mishnah refers to the bringing of that small table.

he dips the lettuce[3]	מְטַבֵּל בַּחֲזֶרֶת.
before he reaches	עַד שֶׁמַּגִּיעַ
the *parpares*[4] of the bread.	לְפַרְפֶּרֶת הַפַּת
They brought before him[1]	הֵבִיאוּ לְפָנָיו
matzoh and lettuce,[5]	מַצָּה וַחֲזֶרֶת
charoses[6] and two cooked dishes,[7]	וַחֲרֹסֶת וּשְׁנֵי תַבְשִׁילִין
although	אַף־עַל־פִּי
the *charoses* is not a *mitzvah*.[8]	שֶׁאֵין חֲרֹסֶת מִצְוָה,
R' Eliezer the son of R' Zadok	רַבִּי אֱלִיעֶזֶר בֶּן־רַבִּי צָדוֹק
says:	אוֹמֵר,
it is a *mitzvah*.[9]	מִצְוָה.
And at the time of the Temple	וּבַמִּקְדָּשׁ
they brought before him	הָיוּ מְבִיאִים לְפָנָיו
the carcass of the Passover sacrifice.[10]	גּוּפוֹ שֶׁל פֶּסַח:

MISHNAH 4

They pour the second cup for him	(ד) מָזְגוּ־לוֹ כּוֹס שֵׁנִי.
and here the son asks.	וְכָאן הַבֵּן שׁוֹאֵל אָבִיו,
If the son is not able [to ask]	וְאִם אֵין דַּעַת בַּבֵּן,

[3] Into salt water. This, as some other things, was done to awaken the curiosity of the children; as it was strange that vegetables be eaten before the bread of the meal.

[4] There is a difference of opinions as to the meaning of פַּרְפֶּרֶת: a) "the breaking of the matzoh," i.e. nothing else is eaten between the dipped vegetable and the matzoh.—(R' *Chananel*) b) "the appetizer," i.e. the *maror*—bitter herbs which are eaten to whet the appetite. The mishnah teaches that although he used lettuce, which is acceptable for *maror*, as the first vegetable, he must dip it again after eating the matzoh, to fulfill the mitzvah of *maror*.— *Rashbam*

[5] For the mitzvah of *maror*.

[6] A dip for the *maror* made from nuts, dates, apples, other fruits and wine mixed to the consistency of mortar as a remembrance of the slave labor to which we were subjected in Egypt.

[7] It is only to lessen the sharpness of the *maror*.

[8] One as a remembrance for the קָרְבַּן פֶּסַח—the Passover sacrifice, and one as a remembrance to the קָרְבַּן חֲגִיגָה—festival offering.

[9] And a *brocho* should be recited. We do not abide by this opinion.

[10] To fulfill the *mitzvah* of eating the קָרְבַּן פֶּסַח along with the קָרְבַּן חֲגִיגָה.

his father teaches him[1]:	אָבִיו מְלַמְּדוֹ.
Why was this night made different	מַה־נִּשְׁתַּנָּה הַלַּיְלָה הַזֶּה
from all [other] nights:	מִכָּל־הַלֵּילוֹת.
that on all [other] nights	שֶׁבְּכָל־הַלֵּילוֹת
we eat either leavened bread or matzoh,	אָנוּ אוֹכְלִין חָמֵץ וּמַצָּה,
[whereas] on this night	הַלַּיְלָה הַזֶּה
only matzo.	כֻּלּוֹ מַצָּה.
On all [other] nights	שֶׁבְּכָל־הַלֵּילוֹת
we eat all kinds of vegetables	אָנוּ אוֹכְלִין שְׁאָר יְרָקוֹת,
[whereas] on this night—maror.	הַלַּיְלָה הַזֶּה מָרוֹר.
On all [other] nights	שֶׁבְּכָל־הַלֵּילוֹת
we eat roasted meat,	אָנוּ אוֹכְלִין בָּשָׂר צָלִי
overcooked or cooked	שָׁלוּק וּמְבֻשָּׁל,
[whereas] on this night, only roasted.[2]	הַלַּיְלָה הַזֶּה כֻּלּוֹ צָלִי.
On all [other] nights	שֶׁבְּכָל־הַלֵּילוֹת
we dip but once[3]	אָנוּ מַטְבִּילִין פַּעַם אַחַת,
[whereas] on this night—twice.[4]	הַלַּיְלָה הַזֶּה שְׁתֵּי פְעָמִים.
According to the ability of the son	וּלְפִי דַעְתּוֹ שֶׁל־בֵּן
his father teaches him.	אָבִיו מְלַמְּדוֹ.
He begins[5] [relating] with [our] shame[6]	מַתְחִיל בִּגְנוּת
and ends with [our] praise.[7]	וּמְסַיֵּם בְּשֶׁבַח,

[1] The reasons for the *mitzvos* and customs of the *Seder*.

[2] The קָרְבָּן פֶּסַח must be roasted (v. chap. 2 Mishnah 5). Of course, this question was asked only at the time of the Temple when we had the קָרְבָּן פֶּסַח.

[3] The text of the Passover Haggadah has another version: "We do not dip *even* once."

[4] Once, the vegetable we eat before the matzoh into salt water; and a second time, when we dip the *maror* into *charoses*. [Nowadays, when there is no question concerning the קָרְבָּן פֶּסַח, we substitute another question concerning the fact that we eat מְסוּבִּין—in a reclining position.—(*Passover Haggadah*)

[5] The *mitzvah* of relating the story of the Exodus from Egypt.

[6] That our forefathers (Terach, father of Abraham) were idol-worshippers and that we started as slaves in Egypt.

[7] That God took us out of Egypt and gave us the *Torah*.

And clarifies	וְדוֹרֵשׁ
[from the verse]	
"Aramea destroyed my father. . ." (Deut. 26:5)	מֵאֲרַמִּי אֹבֵד אָבִי
until he concludes	עַד־שֶׁיִּגְמֹר
the entire Portion.[8]	כָּל־הַפָּרָשָׁה כֻּלָּהּ:

MISHNAH 5

Rabbon Gamliel would often say:	(ה) רַבָּן גַּמְלִיאֵל הָיָה אוֹמֵר,
Whoever has not said[1]	כָּל־שֶׁלֹּא אָמַר
the following three things	שְׁלֹשָׁה דְבָרִים אֵלּוּ
on Pesach	בַּפֶּסַח,
has not fulfilled his obligation	לֹא יָצָא יְדֵי־חוֹבָתוֹ,
and they are:	וְאֵלּוּ הֵן,
Pesach, matzoh, and maror.	פֶּסַח מַצָּה וּמָרוֹר.
[The reason for the] Pesach [sacrifice] is	פֶּסַח,
because God passed	עַל־שׁוּם שֶׁפָּסַח הַמָּקוֹם
over the houses of our forefathers	עַל בָּתֵּי אֲבוֹתֵינוּ
in Egypt.[2]	בְּמִצְרָיִם.
[The reason for] matzoh [is]	מַצָּה,
that our forefathers were redeemed	עַל־שׁוּם שֶׁנִּגְאֲלוּ אֲבוֹתֵינוּ
in Egypt.[3]	מִמִּצְרָיִם.
[The reason for] maror [is]	מָרוֹר,
because the Egyptians made bitter	עַל־שׁוּם שֶׁמֵּרְרוּ הַמִּצְרִים
the lives of our forefathers	אֶת־חַיֵּי אֲבוֹתֵינוּ
in Egypt.[4]	בְּמִצְרָיִם.

[8] Until v. 8. These verses are elaborately explained in the Passover Haggadah.

[1] I.e. he has not stated the reasons for . . .

[2] During the tenth plague—when all the Egyptian first-born were smitten—God passed over our houses and spared our first-born.

[3] Based on the verse (Exodus 12:39): "And they baked the dough that they took from Egypt, loaves of matzos, but not leavened."

[4] End of Rabbon Gamliel's statement.

In every generation	בְּכָל־דּוֹר וָדוֹר
a person is obligated	חַיָּב אָדָם
to see himself,	לִרְאוֹת אֶת־עַצְמוֹ,
as if he himself left Egypt	כְּאִלּוּ הוּא יָצָא מִמִּצְרַיִם.
as it is written:	שֶׁנֶּאֱמַר:
"And you shall relate to your son	וְהִגַּדְתָּ לְבִנְךָ
on that day saying:	בַּיּוֹם הַהוּא לֵאמֹר,
It is for this	בַּעֲבוּר זֶה
that God did for me in Egypt."	עָשָׂה יְיָ לִי בְּצֵאתִי מִמִּצְרַיִם.
Therefore, we are obligated	לְפִיכָךְ אֲנַחְנוּ חַיָּבִים,
to give thanks	לְהוֹדוֹת
to praise, to extoll	לְהַלֵּל לְשַׁבֵּחַ
to glorify, to exalt,	לְפָאֵר לְרוֹמֵם
to declare the splendor, to bless,	לְהַדֵּר לְבָרֵךְ
to raise up, and to laud	לְעַלֵּה וּלְקַלֵּס,
to the One who performed	לְמִי שֶׁעָשָׂה
for our forefathers and for us	לַאֲבוֹתֵינוּ וְלָנוּ
all these miracles;	אֶת־כָּל־הַנִּסִּים הָאֵלּוּ,
he removed us	הוֹצִיאָנוּ
from slavery to freedom,	מֵעַבְדוּת לְחֵרוּת,
from lament to joy	מִיָּגוֹן לְשִׂמְחָה,
and from mourning to *Yom Tov*	וּמֵאֵבֶל לְיוֹם־טוֹב,
and from darkness	וּמֵאֲפֵלָה
to a great light	לְאוֹר גָּדוֹל,
and from subjugation	וּמִשִּׁעְבּוּד
to redemption	לִגְאֻלָּה,
and we say before him, *Hallelujah!*[5]	וְנֹאמַר לְפָנָיו הַלְלוּיָהּ:

---

[5] I.e. we shall recite the *Hallel*—these words preface the Hallel which begins with Psalms chap. 113.

MISHNAH 6

Until where does he say[1] [the *Hallel*]	(ו) עַד הֵיכָן הוּא אוֹמֵר?
Beth Shammai say:	בֵּית־שַׁמַּי אוֹמְרִים,
up to "Eym habanim s'mecho"[2]	עַד אֵם הַבָּנִים שְׂמֵחָה.
and Beth Hillel say:	וּבֵית־הִלֵּל אוֹמְרִים,
up to "Chalomish l'mayno moyim"[3]	עַד חַלָּמִישׁ לְמַעְיְנוֹ מָיִם.
and he closes with [a *brocho*]	וְחוֹתֵם
for redemption.	בִּגְאֻלָּה.
R' Tarfon says:	רַבִּי טַרְפוֹן אוֹמֵר,
[the text of this *brocho* is:]	
"that he redeemed us	אֲשֶׁר גְּאָלָנוּ
and redeemed our forefathers	וְגָאַל אֶת־אֲבוֹתֵינוּ
from Egypt"	מִמִּצְרַיִם
and he does not close [with a *brocho*].[4]	וְאֵינוֹ חוֹתֵם,
R' Akiva says: [that he adds:]	רַבִּי עֲקִיבָא אוֹמֵר:
So, too, shall Hashem, our God	כֵּן יְיָ אֱלֹהֵינוּ
and the God of our forefathers,	וֵאלֹהֵי אֲבוֹתֵינוּ,
allow us to reach	יַגִּיעֵנוּ
to other holidays and festivals	לְמוֹעֲדִים וְלִרְגָלִים אֲחֵרִים,
that are coming towards us	הַבָּאִים לִקְרָאתֵנוּ
at peace,	לְשָׁלוֹם,
happy at the building of Your city	שְׂמֵחִים בְּבִנְיַן עִירֶךָ,
and rejoicing in Your service	וְשָׂשִׂים בַּעֲבוֹדָתֶךָ,
and we shall eat there	וְנֹאכַל שָׁם
from the [*chagiga*] sacrifices	מִן הַזְּבָחִים
and from the Passover sacrifices etc."	וּמִן־הַפְּסָחִים כו'

[1] At the *seder* Hallel is begun before the meal and completed afterwards.

[2] The end of Psalm 113.

[3] The end of Psalm 114. Beth Hillel add בְּצֵאת יִשְׂרָאֵל מִמִּצְרַיִם so that the Exodus and the Splitting of the Red Sea be mentioned. Beth Shammai hold that since the actual Exodus took place at midnight, it should first be mentioned after the meal.

[4] Although he *does* begin with *brocho*, "...בָּרוּךְ אַתָּה ה' אֱלֹקֵינוּ מֶלֶךְ הָעוֹלָם אֲשֶׁר גְּאָלָנוּ.

up to "Blessed are You Hashem עַד בָּרוּךְ אַתָּה יְיָ

Who has redeemed Israel."[5] גָּאַל יִשְׂרָאֵל:

MISHNAH 7 *

They pour for him the third cup, (ז) מָזְגוּ־לוֹ כוֹס שְׁלִישִׁי,

[and] he says Bircas Hamazon.[1] מְבָרֵךְ עַל מְזוֹנוֹ.

[On the] fourth [cup], רְבִיעִי,

he completes the Hallel,[2] גּוֹמֵר עָלָיו אֶת־הַהַלֵּל,

and he recites on it the brocho over song.[3] וְאוֹמֵר עָלָיו בִּרְכַּת הַשִּׁיר.

Between these cups[4] בֵּין הַכּוֹסוֹת הַלָּלוּ,

if he wishes he may drink [wine]; אִם רוֹצֶה לִשְׁתּוֹת יִשְׁתֶּה,

between the third [cup] and the fourth [cup] בֵּין שְׁלִישִׁי לָרְבִיעִי

he may not drink.[5] לֹא יִשְׁתֶּה:

MISHNAH 8

And we don't complete (ח) אֵין מַפְטִירִין

after [the eating of] the Pesach [sacrifice] אַחַר הַפֶּסַח

[with the eating of] desserts.[1] אֲפִיקוֹמָן.

---

[5] R' Akiva adds: 1) the wish that we attain our future redemption and 2)the closing of the prayer with a brocho.

* At this time he has completed the Haggadah, has drunk the second cup, has washed n'tilas yadayim, eaten matzoh and maror and completed his meal.

[1] The blessings after a meal which is recited over a cup of wine.

[2] See previous mishnah where we learned that he says part of hallel before the meal. He now completes the hallel.

[3] The Talmud cites two opinions as to what Bircas Hashir is: a) נִשְׁמַת כָּל חַי b) יְהַלְלוּךְ. Our custom is to say both (see Haggadah).

[4] I.e. the first three cups, for wine drunk during the meal is not intoxicating.

[5] Because once he has completed his meal, wine has a greater tendency to intoxicate and he may not be able to complete the hallel.

[1] מַפְטִירִין, most commentaries hold is derived from the root פטר—to take leave, to end. אפיקומן—most commentaries hold, comes from the Greek "epikontum, epigeima" = lit. the meal after the meal, i.e. desserts. Accordingly, the statement teaches not to eat anything after the Passover sacrifice because the mitzvah of the Pesach requires that it be eaten עַל הַשֹּׂבַע—

If part [of the group] fell asleep,	יָשְׁנוּ מִקְצָתָן,
[upon waking] they may [continue] to eat.	יֹאכֵלוּ,
[If] all [of the group] fell asleep	כֻּלָּם
they may not continue to eat.[2]	לֹא יֹאכֵלוּ.
R' Yose says:	רַבִּי יוֹסֵי אוֹמֵר,
If they dozed off	נִתְנַמְנְמוּ,
they may [continue to] eat.	יֹאכֵלוּ,
If they fell into a deep sleep	נִרְדְּמוּ
they may not [continue to] eat.[3]	לֹא יֹאכֵלוּ:

MISHNAH 9

The Passover Sacrifice after midnight	(ט) הַפֶּסַח אַחַר חֲצוֹת,
ritually contaminates the hands.[1]	מְטַמֵּא אֶת־הַיָּדָיִם.
A putrified sacrifice[2]	הַפִּגּוּל
and the remains of a sacrifice[3]	וְהַנּוֹתָר
ritually contaminate the hands.	מְטַמְּאִין אֶת־הַיָּדָיִם.

---

when satiated. According to some opinions in the *Gemara* this law applies nowadays as well. Though we now have no *Pesach* sacrifice, it is a mitzvah to eat a כזית (olive sized piece) of matzoh after which no other food may be eaten, so that the taste of matzoh remains with us after the *seder*. We, therefore, call this piece of matzoh—the *Afikomen*.

[2] The קרבן פסח—Pesach sacrifice must be eaten in one place (see Pesachim chap. 7, Mishnah 13). Thus, if the entire group fell asleep and interrupted the eating of the Pesach, they cannot, upon waking, continue to eat, for it would be considered eating in two places. However, as long as part of the group remains awake and continues to eat, it is not considered an interruption and those who wake may continue to eat.

[3] R' Yose holds that only if the part of the group dozed (see note 2) may they continue to eat, but if they fell completely asleep they may not continue even if part of the group remained awake.

[1] The Pesach must be consumed by midnight. In order to discourage any of the meat being left after midnight, the Sages decreed that any such meat will render the hands of one who touches it as טָמֵא—ritually unclean.

[2] If at the time of any of the main services of the sacrifices, he had it in mind to eat the sacrifices other than during the specified time or proper place.

[3] If they were left beyond the time alloted to eating them.

If he has recited a *brocho*	בֵּרַךְ
[on] the Pesach sacrifice,	בִּרְכַּת הַפֶּסַח,
he has exempted the *chagiga* sacrifice.	פָּטַר אֶת שֶׁל־זֶבַח,
If he has recited a *brocho* on the *chagiga*,	בֵּרַךְ אֶת שֶׁל־זֶבַח,
he has not exempted the Passover sacrifice:[4]	לֹא פָטַר אֶת־שֶׁל־פֶּסַח,
[these are] the words of R' Yishmael.	דִּבְרֵי רַבִּי יִשְׁמָעֵאל.
Rabbi Akiva says:	רַבִּי עֲקִיבָא אוֹמֵר,
this one does not exempt that one	לֹא זוֹ פוֹטֶרֶת זוֹ,
and that one does not exempt this one.[5]	וְלֹא זוֹ פוֹטֶרֶת זוֹ:

---

[4] (V. *Pesachim* chap. 6, Mishnah 3). Before the קרבן פסח, it is a mitzvah to eat the Chagigah sacrifice. Each one of these two mitzvos has its own *brocho,* i.e. the *chagiga:* בָּרוּךְ אַתָּה ה' אֱלֹקֵינוּ ... and for the פֶּסַח קָרְבָּן: מֶלֶךְ הָעוֹלָם אֲשֶׁר קִדְּשָׁנוּ בְּמִצְוֹתָיו וְצִוָּנוּ לֶאֱכֹל הַזֶּבַח R'. בָּרוּךְ ... וְצִוָּנוּ לֶאֱכוֹל הַפֶּסַח קָרְבָּן: Yishmael holds that since the קָרְבָּן פֶּסַח is the major *mitzvah* of the two, therefore, he can recite the *brocho* on the Pesach for both.

[5] R' Akiva holds that each קָרְבָּן requires its own *brocho.*